TAKING
MIRACLES
SERIOUSLY

TAKING MIRACLES SERIOUSLY

A Journey to Everyday Spirituality

RABBI MICHAEL ZEDEK

SUTHERLAND HOUSE

TORONTO, 2023

Sutherland House
416 Moore Ave., Suite 205
Toronto, ON M4G 1C9

First edition, September 2023

If you are interested in inviting one of our authors to a live event or media appearance, please contact sranasinghe@sutherlandhousebooks.com and visit our website at sutherlandhousebooks.com for more information about our authors and their schedules.

We acknowledge the support of the Government of Canada.

Manufactured in India
Cover designed by Lena Yang
Book composed by Karl Hunt

Library and Archives Canada Cataloguing in Publication
Title: Taking miracles seriously : a journey to
everyday spirituality / Rabbi Michael Zedek.
Names: Zedek, Michael, author.
Description: Includes bibliographical references.
Identifiers: Canadiana (print) 20230184537 | Canadiana (ebook) 20230184626 |
ISBN 9781990823121 (softcover) | ISBN 9781990823145 (EPUB)
Subjects: LCSH: Spiritual life. | LCSH: Religious life.
Classification: LCC BL624 .Z43 2023 | DDC 204/.4—dc23

ISBN 978-1-990823-12-1
eBook 978-1-990823-14-5

To Karen, for the miracle she is and for the miracles we share.

Permissions

Yehuda Amichai, "Psalm," from the *Selected Poetry of Yehuda Amichai*, translated by Chana Bloch, the University of California Press, 2013.

The Midrash Says: The Book of Vayikra, from the Art Scroll series y Moshe Weissman. Used by permission of Bnay Yakov Publications. Copyright 1982.

Wendell Berry ["I go among the trees and sit still] from *This Day: Collected and New Sabbath Poems 1979-2012*. Copyright @ 1979 by Wendell Berry. Reprinted with the permission of The Permissions Company, LLC on behalf of Counterpoint Press, counterpoint.com.

"The Guest House," from *The Essential Rumi*, translated by Coleman Banks, Harper Collins. Copyright @ 1995 by Coleman Banks. Used by permission Mr. Banks.

"Between the conscious and the unconscious," from *Kabir: Ecstatic Poems* by Robert Bly. Copyright @ 2004 by Robert Bly. Reprinted by permission of Beacon Press, Boston.

"A Kingdom of Joy and Awe" by Cham Stern from *Gates of Prayer: The New Union Prayer Book* (p 216) @ 1975 by Central Conference of American Rabbis. Used by permission of the CCAR. All rights reserved.

Contents

Foreword

NOTICE, PLEASE, THIS ONE characteristic of Michael Zedek's experience and writing: he is a practiced and practicing *noticer*. Without ever being didactic about this, he shows that he wants *you* to be a noticer, both of his work and, after reading it, of countless easy-to-be-overlooked, but truly revealing, features of what surrounds us or informs us. Seldom do I read and appraise a manuscript which alerts me as consistently and persuasively as does the one which became this book, to notice that which may be hidden or ignored and to express hope that readers will be motivated to improve their own "noticing" quotient and capability.

The concept of noticing, which the dictionary defines as "becoming aware of . . . something or someone," is ceaseless, a constant in life—even when one is dreaming. It can be so taken for granted that its potential for enhancing life can easily be overlooked. But it deserves notice.

Let me take a moment to locate the concept of "being a noticer" in a literary context. The great English poet, Thomas Hardy, devoted his best-known poem "Afterwords" to reflection on his own role as a noticer. When he wrote, Hardy was seventy-seven years old, unsure whether he would publish again. (He lived eleven more years.) His lines concentrated on very quiet and subtle realities to which he paid attention: thus when "the May month flaps its wings, delicate-filmed as some new-spun silk," he asks, "Will the neighbours say, 'He was a man who used to notice such things?'"

We become his virtual neighbors, as we read him writing that after his passing they would say, "He was one who had an eye for . . . mysteries." To notice "mysteries" and subtleties was the vocation of the great poet.

Noticing and finding ways to communicate mysteries in what he saw and heard and felt is also the vocation of Rabbi Zedek. You could look that assignment up in any seminary manuals for future rabbis. One notices, it is intended also to be part of the vocation of those who make up the rabbi's congregations or of others in the culture, who become aware of his vocation and achievement.

To speak in these terms might suggest that this book is a flittery New Age work without a focus or clear intentions. Notice: without ever sounding polemical or didactic, Rabbi Zedek could not be more focused, clear, or grounded as when he plunks down a sentence like this about his intentions: "I hope this book reminds us that we need not wait for the exceptional moments in order to realize how remarkable this world and our lives are, even if we cannot hold them close enough." Always aware of the lives of us readers, the rabbi shows that he knows that few of us can live dramatically at the mountain. "No, there are full diapers and traffic delays, distractions, and disappointments galore. Any number of mundane, routine matters fill our days. . . . (In short,) every event points to an ultimate reality, as you'd likely expect a religious person to insist, behind everything is the One, the infinite, or to use the traditional Western word, God."

Zedek elaborates and clarifies the matter by quoting my fellow Nebraskan Willa Cather: "Miracles . . . seem to me to rest not so much upon faces or voices or healing power coming suddenly near to us from afar off, but upon our perceptions being made finer, so that for a moment our eyes can see and our ears can hear what is there about us always."

Rabbi Zedek, our light-hearted and never overbearing sage, bids in Chapter 2, "Let's talk," which he does, and we listen and then also are ready more than before to talk about mysteries in and about ordinary life.

by Dr. Martin Marty, Professor Emeritus,
The University of Chicago

INTRODUCTION

Is That All There Is?

I T'S A SAFE BET that as you read this book, somewhere in North America a high school drama group is either preparing for or currently performing Thornton Wilder's *Our Town*.[1] Although almost a century old, the play retains its power to stir. It also serves as something of an introduction to the vagaries of life for many of the young people who read it, view it, or stage it.

You may recall the scene in which a distraught Emily, having just revisited her twelfth birthday, insists on returning to the cemetery: "up the hill—to my grave." As she departs, Emily offers a lament and a challenge: "Oh, earth, you're too wonderful for anybody to realize you." Turning to the stage manager, she inquires, "Do any human beings ever realize life while they live it—every, every minute?" The stage manager's initial response is an unadorned "No." But after a brief pause, he adds, "Saints and poets maybe—they do some."

Emily's is a provocative and searching question. Who wouldn't mind "realizing" more of life, if only it didn't require the inconvenience, time, and character necessary for poetry or sainthood?

While this book does not pretend to be a guide for either calling, it does embrace the conviction that there are teachings, stories, suggestions, and actions that may assist us more fully to realize, embrace, and rejoice in the gift of life—more specifically, the gift of our lives. Surely, we are able to recall some overwhelming and awesome moment, perhaps even an experience of a sacred dimension, a time when life resonates with a clarity that surpasses words. At such times, we understand the poet Edna St. Vincent Millay's declaration, "O World, I cannot hold thee close enough!"[2]

With that intimacy in mind, I hope this book reminds us that we need not wait for exceptional moments in order to realize how remarkable this world and our lives are, even if we cannot hold them close enough. For few are those with the time and stamina or, for that matter, the assistants and money to live at the mountaintop of peak experiences. No, there are full diapers and traffic delays, distractions, and disappointments galore. Any number of mundane, routine matters fill our days. For many of us, Peggy Lee's "Is that all there is?" is the more familiar utterance.[3]

Yet we yearn for Lee's lyric to be wrong. Its mournful question need not be the bottom line. In fact, the insights of many sacred traditions dispute that claim. The religious imagination insists not only that the exceptional and the extraordinary—those so-called mountaintop moments—are evidence of something more but also that the commonplace may be elevated to the realm of spiritual adventure.

I do not ignore the obvious. Our world is broken in too many places and for too many of us. My Jewish tradition is not alone in the conviction that our job, for as long as the breath of life resides in us, is to do something about that. We are meant to close at least some of the distance between the world as it is and the world as it should be, even if that only means just a little more kindness, justice, and mercy.

E. B. White expresses the tension perfectly. "I arise in the morning torn between a desire to save the world and a desire to savor the world. This makes it hard to plan the day."[4] I am convinced that were we able to savor the world more fully and embrace it as it is, we would enhance our ability to heal it. Were we open to miracles of the ordinary, we also would discover that we are part of a sacred dimension that, even as it calls us to action, is always present, always around and in us. Simply put, if we were less inclined to take the ordinary for granted, our lives would be filled with more living, with more life. And, as White elaborates, "if we forget to savor the world, what possible reason do we have for saving it?"

The supremely worthwhile goal of bridging the gulf between saving and savoring may be pursued and embraced by exploring commonplace paths to a sacred dimension. By cultivating an awareness of and sensitivity to holiness and a more-than-words encounter with an essential spirit, we have the capacity to become more alive and whole. An embrace of the sacred may take us to the very heart of a meaningful life.

A true and lasting encounter with holiness does not require an invariably difficult discipline, or secret wisdom, or deep access to an individual or collective consciousness. Rather, we may find, see, and experience holiness regularly and well. The inimitable Sherlock Holmes offers a comment that sets our course: "I've trained myself to notice what I see."[5]

I understand that many of us have had experiences with religion and its adherents who seem to conflate serious ideas with a severe affect. Philip Roth's description of the Rabbi who pronounced "God" as though it were a three-syllable word comes to mind.[6] While I cannot deny that experience, I intend to offer something more nuanced, or elastic, as we examine material from a number of sacred traditions, as well as stories, illustrations, and examples from a range of sources from the ancient to the contemporary. Whether you are an adherent of a religious tradition or far removed from any such embrace, I hope to demonstrate that there is no place where the sacred is absent.

You may find some of what I have to say anachronistic, unorthodox, irreverent, or even heretical. I hope you will remain open, regardless, to reframing concepts of miracles, God, prayer, and poetry, even if you have previously discarded them. A serious encounter with the sacred requires, at least, a confrontation with those topics. So nothing is off limits here. I am convinced that a new or renewed contact with familiar ideas can enrich us as we explore the heart of living. At the same time, I acknowledge the possibility of being wrong. As Voltaire said, "Doubt is an uncomfortable condition, but certainty is absurd."[7]

My hope, should you decide to take this journey with me, is that you will come to agree that the answer to Peggy Lee's despairing refrain is a resounding "No." What there is, is more than enough to lead us to a far more joyful conclusion.

PART 1

Taking Miracles Seriously

The extraordinary moments in our lives—the birth of a child, the loss of a loved one, falling in love, deep friendships—require little from us in order to grab our attention. We cannot but notice. Metaphorically, they slap us across the face and insist we take note. And unless we are among the most jaded, we do. But the key to transforming our lives from a saga whose pages are filled with an endless and largely unsatisfying pursuit of thrills, grand moments, and exceptional experiences lies in reframing the repetitive, mundane, routine, difficult, and even tragic moments so that we see them as spiritual adventures or, as I prefer to call them, miracles of the ordinary.

CHAPTER 1

A Secret Hiding in Plain Sight

Exploring biblical stories about miracles, in a serious but not literal way, can help us recognize that we live in a miracle-infused world.

I ONCE HEARD THE MUCH-ADMIRED minister, Dr. Fred Craddock,[1] describe a trip to Israel during which his guide pointed to a location as the setting of some specific miracle. Craddock demurred with a polite "I hope you don't mind if I understand the experience differently." Without missing a beat, the guide immediately responded, "Of course not. You can be sure if there is only one way to interpret something, it didn't come from God."

The guide's comment perfectly conveys a way of thinking about sacred texts that resides at the heart of my tradition, which happens to be Judaism.[2] It is captured in two Hebrew words, *Dvar Acher*, literally translated as "another word" or "thing." It means another interpretation, not a better or worse one, not the right instead of your wrong one, just another way of seeing, of understanding, and of wrestling with the text and life's circumstances.

In effect, to understand the stories of the Hebrew Bible only literally guarantees we shall miss their meaning, or more precisely, the meanings in them and the lessons they convey. We take the text far too seriously to take it only literally. Simply put, biblical narratives and those in other traditions, especially ones that include the miraculous, are different and more complex than they may appear to be.

Indian folklore includes a tale of a guru whose ambition was somehow to impress the Buddha. The man determined to walk on water, convinced that doing so would gain him the attention he sought. For twenty years, he practiced intense meditation and total, disciplined mindfulness. According to the story, he did it. He walked on water. The guru demonstrated his skill to the Buddha, who asked, "Why didn't you just pay two rupees and take the ferry?"

There is an American folktale involving a hunter who, excited to test his newly acquired dog, loaded his truck and took the animal to a favorite duck pond. He shot a bird and instructed the dog to fetch. The dog obliged, but rather than swimming, the animal walked out on the water to retrieve the duck. Taken aback, the hunter packed his truck and rushed back to town. The next day, the hunter invited a friend to join him at the duck pond. Once again, a duck was shot, and the dog walked on water to retrieve the prey. Neither man said a word. Finally, the hunter could no longer restrain himself. "You notice anything peculiar about my dog?" he asked his friend. After some hesitation, the friend replied: "Come to think of it, yeah. The darn thing doesn't know how to swim."

These stories reflect an irony that repeats in the Hebrew Bible, with its plethora of *miracle* tales. Every time a miracle occurs, no one draws the "correct" lesson.

Some readers will recall *Mister Ed*, a situation comedy from the golden age of television. It featured a talking horse by that name, who introduced himself to his new owner by exclaiming, in an unmistakable baritone, "Willbuurrr." Wilbur (played by Alan Young) was appropriately dumbstruck. It is not in our experience to have animals speak, let alone deliver punchlines, even in classic situation comedies. Yet the Bible has a precedent in the story of Balaam and his ass.[3] The difference is that Balaam evidences no hesitation or surprise in his business-as-usual conversation with a donkey. Shouldn't we expect to a more reasonable response, one not unlike Wilbur's? Wouldn't Wilbur's reaction be our own?

Even more puzzling are the Ten Plagues of Egypt.[4] There have been many attempts to explain the plagues, from timely natural phenomena and Pharaoh's hard heart to supernatural interventions, but the bigger question is, why does it take ten of them to convince Pharaoh to let the Israelites go? One would have been enough to convince you or me.

In Cecil B. DeMille's 1956 movie version of the biblical story,[5] Dothan, played by Edward G. Robinson, sees in the distance the dust cloud of the Egyptian chariots. He thunders at Moses, played by Charlton Heston, "Why did you bring us out here to die? Weren't there enough graves in Egypt?" That theme echoes throughout the Exodus story, as the Israelites default to a repetitive and limited repertoire of responses—panicking and complaining, griping and moaning. But why? Don't they realize that God is playing for their team? Why don't they recognize that the Egyptians chasing them are suicidal fools?

As Moses tries to calm the Israelites, he turns to Deity who, the text says,[6] responds to Moses' plea to work some "magic" with an unexpected and, for my purposes instructive, "Why do you cry out to Me? Tell the children of Israel to go forward."

That the people actually comply may be the real miracle. They go forward. As you likely recall, the text informs us that the sea splits and the children of Israel walk through on dry ground. So that is not one miracle. It is at least two. What happened to the mud? A further consideration, were you an Egyptian chariot driver, would you follow the Israelites in? Of course not. You would have to be crazy. Yet, according to the text, that is precisely what they do: "And then the Israelites beheld Egypt[7] dead at the shores of the sea."

More critically, we then read, "The Israelites believed in God and in Moses, God's servant." That only lasts until the next chapter when they echo Dothan's grievance: "Why did you bring us out here to die? We have no water," a matter Moses addresses by striking a rock from which water gushes forth.

The water-from-a-rock "miracle" is available to any tourist in Sinai. A guide may hand you a geology hammer and a piece of limestone, one of the principal rock formations of the area. Splitting the rock may reveal the hollowing effect of a modest bit of accumulated moisture. Not quite enough water to slacken the thirst of twelve tribes and livestock, it at least offers a provocative basis for the biblical story.

Things are calm as order is restored but, alas, only for a few verses. Now the crisis is a lack of food. So the Israelites are provided manna, which must be one of the more subtle moments of humor in Hebrew Scripture. The text informs us they called it manna, which is an extension of their declaration upon beholding this mysterious stuff: "*Mann hu?*" they inquire. "What is it?" As if they were handed some variation of mystery meat.

Their hunger is satisfied but not for long. The people grow tired of the same menu and again demonstrate a singular talent for complaint. Death in Egypt was preferable to life without the delights they left behind: leeks, pomegranates, onions, and garlic.

They want, they *demand* meat. And wouldn't you know, the next day the Israelite camp is surrounded by birds. Often imprecisely translated as quail, this "miracle" occurs every year as birds in extraordinary numbers make their semiannual migrations between various parts of Europe and Africa. Since the journey over the Mediterranean provides no opportunity for rest, the relatively uninhabited and undisturbed Sinai Peninsula is where birds often stop to gain strength for the next stage of their journey. If you are in Sinai at that time, you are likely to see enormous flocks of birds. As they recover, they are, as the biblical account describes, practically unable to move.

The pattern is the point. The Israelites panic and complain, gripe and moan their way across the desert. Finally arriving at Mount Sinai, the text informs that God, in what may be categorized as the single greatest personal appearance of all time, speaks to the entire community.[8] Then

Moses ascends the mountain, and the people, as is their default behavior, panic once more and force Aaron to build a golden calf.

Obviously, something is going on—even going wrong. One possible reading leads to the conclusion that the Israelites are the dumbest people ever to walk the face of the earth. How could they experience so many "miracles" yet not draw the seemingly obvious lesson that everything will be alright and that they are safe, guarded, and secure? Perhaps not surprisingly, I take issue with that notion, as it requires a literal reading of the Bible, which is far too limiting of its timeless wisdom.

Dr. Martin Luther King, Jr., offers a deep and subtle alternative— namely, the Exodus drama demonstrates that "it is easier to get the slaves out of Egypt than it is to get Egypt out of the slaves."[9] This is true in the biblical account and of every journey toward freedom, be it a moment of national or personal liberation. What keeps us in chains is often our inability or unwillingness to accept our independence and power. We are free before we may realize and embrace our freedom.

While I have no argument with the accuracy of King's reflection, I propose an additional perspective. I believe there is an alternative and essential lesson for all time and for all people. As the great teacher and friend of Dr. King, Rabbi Abraham Joshua Heschel, remarks, "People are free to disbelieve the evidence of their own experience."[10]

There are few matters about which I am more certain than that statement. True of the ancient Israelites, true for me, and I would venture, at least some of the time, true of all. Or as *Gates of Prayer*, a prayer book of Reform Judaism, reminds, "Days pass. Years vanish and we walk sightless among miracles."

Are there not methods and motifs to gain better sight and greater insight? Part of the challenge may be our notion of what constitutes a miracle. Just about any attempt to offer a definition likely includes reference to a supernatural intervention into the regular and routine of our experience. For some, the idea of a break in the natural order provides the vital attraction and power of these biblical tales. The more skeptical among us find that the same material only leads to the inevitable conclusion that religion is fable and, more likely, a collective fantasy. Curiously, there is no word in Hebrew for that notion of miracle. Biblical Hebrew includes words often translated as miracle, but their core meanings are different and, for our purposes, provocative. Three specific words are "*Nes*," which means banner, flag, or sign; "*Ot*," meaning a letter, symbol, or sign; and "*Peleh*," meaning wonder, marvel, or an amazement.

For biblical tradition, then, the notion of miracles as discrete supernatural events may be understood as an illusion, one that may blind us to the allusions of a miraculous and sacred presence, one which is around us and in us always. For what isn't a sign, wonder, and amazement? What doesn't point to something else, something more? As mystical tradition and equally much of modern physics insist, there is a unity behind all appearances, a singularity of energy in which everything that is, is no more than a manifestation. The world and the grain of sand are one, and we "hold infinity in the palm of [the] hand."[11]

Every event points to an ultimate reality (as you'd likely expect a religious person to insist) that behind everything is the One, the infinite, or, to use the traditional Western word, God. For those uncomfortable with that invocation, I ask your forbearance. We will discuss notions of deity in Part 2.

Willa Cather has this to say about our relation to the miraculous in her classic novel *Death Comes for the Archbishop*:[12]

> Miracles . . . seem to me to rest not so much upon faces or voices or healing power coming suddenly near to us from afar off, but upon our perceptions being made finer, so that for a moment our eyes can see and our ears can hear what is there about us always.

Einstein was more precise: "There are only two ways to live. The first is as though nothing is a miracle. The other is as though everything is a miracle."[13] I believe we can make the choice to live that second way.

The dividends on that path are substantial, even incalculable. The journey may transform our lives, whatever their circumstance and condition, into a sacred pilgrimage. But for us to make the journey, we must reorient our notion of the miraculous and recognize what the Hebrew Bible conveys in a seemingly obscure or even esoteric way: there are countless miracles hiding in plain sight. It requires only a new way of seeing and understanding so that we may be present to what is there about us and in us always.

FOR FURTHER REFLECTION:

1. How do you react to the idea that there may be multiple ways to understand the same story or experience?
2. If or when you've had an encounter with a person or persons who may understand the "same" experience or information differently than you, how might you engage in conversation toward resolution or perhaps deeper understanding?
3. What seemingly routine events in your life might be reconsidered as remarkable moments? How might that change the way you live and understand your life?

CHAPTER 2

Moses at the Burning Bush

What we might regard as madness, the biblical story of Moses presents as a key to taking miracles seriously.

I N AN INTERVIEW JUST before his death, the Nobel Prize-winning author Isaac Bashevis Singer said:

> For me everything is still mysterious, even the most natural things. When I throw a stone and it falls back to earth I know that it's gravity, but isn't that a great mystery? Just because you've seen a thing ten times should it stop being mysterious? A writer gave me once a story about a man with a chopped off head who talks. I said, "Isn't it marvelous enough that a man with a head can talk?[1]

So let's talk.

Is it possible to demystify the miracle stories in the Hebrew Bible and still attach value and reverence to them? Is there a notion of miracle that does not require a suspension of disbelief, such that the only options are that Deity acted, in those days, in ways no longer available to us or that the whole biblical framework is filled with fairy tales or, to use an especially apt Yiddish word, "*narisshkeit*"?[2]

The episode of Moses at the burning bush is a preeminent challenge for us. What would we conclude were someone other than Moses to inform us that while out in the desert or in a local park, he or she had seen a bush that was both burning and not burning up and also that the bush spoke to them? Our most likely response would be skepticism or, perhaps to suggest medical attention, or more problematic, to give the person a television show on which to offer prayers in return for our cash pledges.

More seriously, how would one know a bush is burning yet not being consumed? The biblical description defies language, logic, and science. If the bush is burning, then it is, even if slowly, burning up; if it is not burning up, in what sense is it on fire at all?

It might not occur to all of us, on coming upon a burning bush, that it is anything out of the ordinary. It occurred to Moses who, as we read in Exod. 3:3, chose to "turn aside to look at this marvelous sight." That phrase can only mean to pay attention. A normal response upon glimpsing a fire is to assume that something is burning and, short of some intervention, will soon burn up. It requires more than a glance or two to ask as Moses does, "Why doesn't the bush burn up?"[3]

A friend who spent many years as a resident of New England points out that many homes there have a working fireplace. If one were to have a fire roaring away in the hearth, it would take some period of time to notice that the logs were being reduced or consumed. Tongue in cheek, he suggested it takes about seven minutes of paying attention before one might recognize that the logs are undiminished. Perhaps a point of the story, then, is that Moses is Moses (and we are not) because he possesses a greater attention span so that he could stay focused longer than we common folk.

More substantively, and some may find this heterodox, if not heretical, I do not believe bushes talk—in Hebrew, Greek, Latin, or English. But I do think we may hear ourselves addressed and experience a sacred dimension in a multitude of encounters, be they with persons, moments, art, and the environment. In fact, I would argue such is possible with all things and in all experiences.

An ancient Midrash[4] instructs that not a single blade of grass can grow unless the angel for that blade of grass whispers to it, "Grow. Grow."[5] While I do not consider that factual, it conveys a truth. For, surely, we have all experienced moments—a remarkable sunset, a precious exchange between friends, a perfect day, the moment of birth, the death of someone loved—when life conveys a clarity and coherence such that we know, like Moses, "[t]he ground upon which we walk is holy."[6]

The text clearly indicates that Moses experiences something that changes his life. There he is, safe in the Sinai suburbs, married to the boss' daughter, no doubt belonging to all the right clubs, and he throws it all away and puts his life at risk for the sake of a vision and for a people who will rarely be grateful and more commonly will engage in ceaseless bellyaching.

What's the likeliest explanation for what happened to Moses?

Recall, as the text states, it is near sunset in the desert. For us moderns, that means something remarkable and rare, an unpolluted and clear sky, one, as it were, ablaze with color. Moses observes, at least as a possibility, a bush between him and the horizon. Whether the story happened in fact or is only the invention of a storyteller, that bush would have to be a gnarled, thorny, small-leafed shrub, the sort of specialized vegetation adapted to a desert environment. The small leaves minimize evaporation, and the thorns make it difficult for animals to consume the plant.

What Moses sees, then, is a rather unimpressive bramble set before a sky on fire. But what he understands is more critical. Moses realizes that he cannot be indifferent, and cannot be safe, while his people are burning in the furnace of Egyptian slavery.[7] With that conviction, that message or communication, Moses begins the story of one group's liberation, a story that literally continues to inform and change the world.

When we engage in a reasonable and reasoned examination of this episode, by which I mean putting aside the notion of miracles as supernatural interventions, we find revealed an alternative that allows a deep understanding of a miracle close at hand.

FOR FURTHER REFLECTION:

1. Do you recall an experience when, like Moses, you felt yourself addressed in a deep and nuanced fashion?
2. If so, did that encounter cause you to make changes in your life? What were they?

CHAPTER 3

Awakening to Spiritual Treasures

There is nothing that does not belong in the category of miraculous.

A FRIEND HAS AN important reminder framed over her kitchen sink: "Normal day, let me be aware of the treasure you are."[1] That same spirit breathes in an elaboration by Chaim Stern:[2]

O give thanks
that spring will always come
to make the heart leap,
that your winter ear remembers
a summer song,
and autumn colors return
to the jaded eye.

O make song
for lucid air of morning,
bright blood's beating,

life's flow deep and swift,
a kingdom of joy and awe
for us to dwell in.

O be glad
for eye and tongue,
to see and taste
the common of our days.

The final phrase is key. For if we were to grasp more fully the "common of our days" and to embrace and be embraced by an awareness of a sacred dimension that resides in everything, including the common and routine, the result would be our holding life closer, whatever its duration, and a fuller appreciation of every moment.

But so often we bifurcate the world into the artificial categories of natural and supernatural. For many, especially those who call themselves believers, that is a critical division, even while others view the same dichotomy as sufficient to dismiss religion as foolishness and fairy tale.

There is a *Dvar Acher*, another interpretation or option. A simple truth resides at the heart of many traditional teachings as the poets always have known and continue to instruct us: there is nothing *but* miracle.

Reflect on Walt Whitman's perfectly titled poem, *Miracles*.[3]

Why, who makes much of a miracle?
As to me I know of nothing else but miracles,
Whether I walk the streets of Manhattan,
Or dart my sight over the roofs of houses toward the sky . . .
Or stand under trees in the woods,
Or talk by day with any one I love . . .
Or sit at table at dinner with the rest . . .
Or watch honey bees busy around the hive of a summer forenoon,
Or animals feeding in the fields,

Or birds, or the wonderfulness of insects in the air,
Or the wonderfulness of the sundown, or of stars shining so quiet
    and bright . . .
To me every hour of the light and dark is a miracle,
Every cubic inch of space is a miracle . . .
To me the sea is a continual miracle,
The fishes that swim—the rocks—the motion of the waves—the ships
    with men in them,
What stranger miracles are there?

Elizabeth Barrett Browning, even from a wheelchair, understood the awesome quality in the everyday. She reframes and extends Moses' experience at the burning bush:

Earth's crammed with heaven,
And every common bush afire with God;

And only he who sees takes off his shoes;
The rest sit round it and pluck blackberries.[4]

The genius of her reflection is the recognition that one cannot merely pluck blackberries. Even that ought to be a burning bush moment.

There are burning bushes scattered throughout every day. We must ignore at least most of them. The alternative is to wake up, gasp in astonishment, and utter a "Wow" that has no end and leaves no room for any other activity.

That is the thrust of a teaching found in Jewish tradition that one may not walk more than four cubits (about 6 feet) without pausing to give praise to the source of life. There is an obvious tension there: how can one take so long between praises? The disquieting answer, especially for those who claim the label of monotheist, is that in some fashion we are all dualists in our perception of experience. Regardless of one's conviction about the supernatural, we can't help ourselves. We divide experience into two categories: the ordinary and extraordinary.

As to the extraordinary, what we do is as obvious as it is unavoidable. By definition, the extraordinary merits or, better, demands our attention. We cannot but see as, at least metaphorically, the extraordinary slaps us across the face and requires our presence. I am part of the first generation of partners regularly present as witness to the birth of their children. And it never ceases to occur that, with the birth of a healthy infant, witnesses emerge with some beatific refrain, an often exhausted and babbling insistence that they have just participated in a miracle. Yet, objectively, what has happened or changed? The world is still the world we've always known. Problems, both global and personal, remain to challenge any assertion of meaning or miracle. The answer, of course, is that one's awareness, one's mindfulness, has been altered, even as we all know how difficult, if not impossible, it is to abide in or prolong that moment of astonishment.

Our response to the ordinary is similarly predictable. We take it for granted. But, again, were we to take the ordinary for granted less, our lives would be filled with more life. Paying attention, really seeing and experiencing that which in its predictability and routine we hardly notice is key. "Perhaps," offers Rabbi Heschel, "the essential message of [religion] is that in doing the finite we can perceive the infinite."[5] Behind or within every experience, no matter how mundane, is a path to awe, reverence, and wonder. Or, as I am fond of suggesting, it takes no great wisdom to recognize that the *a-ha* moment is incredible. However, to remember, with every moment, that the *ho-hum* can also be *a-ha* opens us to an embrace of life for which no words are sufficient or, perhaps, required.

Judaism, like any number of religious traditions, subtly anchors and promotes that conviction through the discipline of specific and fixed prayers. Among the first devotions studied in rabbinical seminary are initial prayers to greet a new day. One is euphemistically referred to as the "plumber's prayer." A sanitized translation of the Hebrew reads in part:

Praised are You, Eternal our God, Ruler of the Universe, Who has fashioned us in wondrous manner with openings and closings. If that which were to be opened were closed up and that which is closed up were opened, we could not stand before You.[6]

The prayer urges us to acknowledge that obviously essential activities such as urination and defecation, most commonly described in profane terms, are filled with the miraculous, with holiness. The conclusion of the prayer invokes a verb form for one of the words, which is regularly, if imprecisely, translated as miracle. The Hebrew root is *Peleh,* meaning a wonder or something awesome. The verb form used is *Maphlee,* which may be interpreted as one who causes or brings wonder. So, as the Psalmist reminds us, we are "awesomely made."[7] But to recognize that urination and defecation may be understood as spiritual moments clearly expands our definition of the sacred. More commonly, our attention focuses on our bodies only at times of dysfunction, rather than in the remarkable rhythm of consistency that we take for granted. We tend to our health most often when we don't have it. The truth is we are wondrously fashioned. As a sage advises, "Woe to the person who stands on earth and does not see what he sees."[8]

Prayer, art, music, a rainbow, children's laughter, a mother's tears, a friend's embrace, even a visit to the toilet—all and more are moments in which we may recognize that behind appearances there is always, and perhaps only, the infinite or divine. We are surrounded by wonder and miracle. We are never not in the presence of the sacred, whether or not we see. As Marcel Proust reminds us, "The real voyage of discovery consists not in seeking new landscapes but in having new eyes."[9]

A colleague, Rabbi Abraham Twerski, conveyed this idea in a modern commentary:

To children born and raised in the desert, it was perfectly natural for . . . food to fall from the heavens. When they entered the Promised

Land and for the first time saw food growing from the ground, they considered this a wondrous miracle. "You put a seed in the ground, and it actually grows into food, just like the food that regularly fell from the sky."[10]

In fact, bread from the sky is no more a miracle than bread from the earth. And bread from the earth is no less than miraculous.[11] As the late Prime Minister of Israel, David Ben Gurion, used to say, "In this country, if you don't believe in miracles, you're not a realist."

In Israel and everywhere that is true or ought to be. Every step takes us over holy ground. Of course, like the Israelites in the desert, we are free to disbelieve the evidence of our own experience.[12] But if that be so, we are free to believe as well. Or, to reverse a popular observation, some things have to be believed in order to be seen.

How, then, do we embrace a sense of mystery and awe and hear the whisper of the sacred that stands behind or resides within all things? I recall a sunset in the Negev desert of Israel, the sky ablaze in reds and blues, and purple hues beyond the genius of a Cézanne or Matisse. One could only applaud, "Author, Author," or, since I was part of a Jewish group, "Praised are You, Eternal our God whose world is filled with such glory."

Not surprisingly, every serious religious tradition wrestles with the challenge of perception and perspective. As the video artist Bill Viola offered in a lecture I attended, "All spiritual practices begin with retraining the eye to see." In the argot of contemporary spirituality, that translates into frequent references about intention or mindfulness.

Consider a verse in the Book of Exodus. The text records the instruction to Moses, "Go up on the mountain and be there."[13] As it happens, one of the hermeneutic guidelines for Jewish interpretation of sacred literature is that the text contains no extraneous words—hence, the query found in Hasidic[14] tradition: Why does Moses need to be told to "be there"? After all, if he climbs Mount Sinai, where else would he be?

The framing of the question reveals the response. All of us know the experience of being physically present in some setting, even though we aren't really *there*. Instead, we contemplate or worry about a meeting later that afternoon or some disappointment from yesterday. Our thoughts routinely take us on meandering journeys through a wilderness of deadlines, appointments, worries, misgivings, and daydreams; all the while, our physical location does not change.

A story from Zen Buddhism:

> One disciple said, "My master stands on one side of the river. I stand on the other holding a piece of paper. He draws a picture in the air, and the picture appears on the paper. He works miracles."
>
> The other disciple said, "My master works greater miracles than that. When he sleeps, he sleeps. When he eats, he eats. When he works, he works. When he meditates, he meditates."[15]

Simply put, be in the moment, in the present, for then one may experience something of presence, perhaps even a sacred dimension.

Some will remember the late Professor Leo Buscaglia as a longtime fixture of Public Broadcasting Service fundraisers. Described only somewhat tongue in cheek as the "Professor of Love," Buscaglia's appeal had much to do with a joyful eloquence, an exceptional, if optimistic, honesty about self and others and, especially, an apparently inexhaustible ebullience that his body could hardly contain. In one of his televised lectures, he described a trip to Japan that included a visit to a wonderful garden. His guide was an important master of the Zen Buddhist tradition. Buscaglia would not stop commenting about the remarkable beauty of each vista. Every turn in the path evoked some profound insight or reflection. Without warning, the guide, completely silent until then, slapped Buscaglia's face and demanded, "Don't walk in my head with your dirty feet!"[16]

The teaching is to be in the moment, rather than offering thoughts in the unspoken hope or pretense that your erudition will prove your worth.

Experience the experience first. Be present to it and to all that resides within it. There will always be opportunity for reflection, commentary, and critique. To abide in astonishment does not require that the world know how intuitive, poetic, or brilliant we are or presume to be. We need to let the moment course through, over, and in us. We must literally let it be. Thoughts and connections will come. Memories may stir. But we need not convince others of anything. In fact, such efforts only get in the way. As Franz Kafka instructs:

> You do not have to leave the room.
> Remain standing at your table and listen.
> Do not even listen, simply wait.
> Be quite still and solitary.
> The world will freely offer itself to you.
> To be unmasked.
> It has no choice.
> It will roll in ecstasy at your feet.[17]

While it is difficult to reconcile that reflection with the Kafka routinely described as a prophet of alienation, his commentary suggests that no matter how despairing our circumstance, the experience of presence, of mindfulness, of ecstasy is available for all of us. So let's embrace that notion as we awaken to the present and allow the spiritual treasures all around and within to be revealed.

FOR FURTHER REFLECTION:

1. While it is normal to take the routine for granted, what do you imagine might happen were you to reframe such matters as new and remarkable?
2. What stops you from doing so?

CHAPTER 4

What Gets in Our Way?

The mundane moments and frequent challenges of life too often distract, mislead, and prevent us from being fully present to what is around and in us.

THE CHALLENGE FOR US is how to acquire the awareness, the mindfulness we desire. Perhaps it would be best to start by asking what gets in the way?

The answer, of course, is many things or, perhaps more accurately, everything. I shall focus on just a few matters.

The pace and focus of modern life are parts of the challenge. We often possess exceptional skill at making our livings but are far less expert at the more vital matter of making a life. Business and busyness get in the way and, in fact, sometimes serve as substitutes for the meaning and values that lead to a fulfilling life, something more than a sentence to endure. We relentlessly pursue happiness as though it will turn up with the next big purchase or promotion. We confuse or conflate affluence with meaning. We presume success means the right brands, a correct address, exclusive parties, or the perfect vacation. But as Lily Tomlin reminds us, "The trouble with [the] rat race is that even if you win, you're still a rat."[1]

Then, too, we want what we want, and we insist on being gratified without delay. Since patience cannot be purchased, we have little to spare. As the late rock-and-roll icon Jim Morrison sang, "We want the world, and we want it now."[2]

Our rationalization and complaint departments are filled with endless variations on "I tried meditation for several days, how come I haven't achieved enlightenment already?" Or, "I worked out hard for twenty minutes a day for a whole week, why don't I have rock-hard abs?"

A *New Yorker* cartoon by Bruce Eric Kaplan shows a couple at the beach, enjoying their preferred adult beverages, as one says to the other, "This is perfect. I could stay like this for the next five seconds."[3]

Yet any serious pilgrimage for spiritual growth requires time and effort. We may desire the outcome, but we excuse our indolence: "As soon as I accumulate [insert some preconceived and often increasing amount of net worth], I'll have sufficient assets to devote time to growth in character, to matters of the spirit. Right now, I'm too busy. I don't have the time. Speak with my assistant."

Or perhaps you have heard something like this: "When I finally overcome the [substance abuse, ruinous relationship, or some other neurotic or self-defeating behavior] that keeps me at an emotional dead end, I'll finally have my act together. Then I'll be ready for some spiritual growth."

We postpone the very activities and actions that will relieve the circumstances that keep us trapped in a cycle of somnolence or, even more problematic, despair.

These traps reinforce the wisdom that it is easier to act one's way into right thinking than to think one's way into right acting. Rather than waiting for the just-so-perfect moment, we need to act with the conviction that we must change our lives if we are to change our lives at all.

That leads to what I believe is the principal obstacle to personal growth or, more immediately, to this effort to see and embrace experience with new eyes—namely, we aren't sufficiently comfortable in our own skins, and we too often sabotage ourselves.

In words that sound remarkably current, St. Augustine gives anguished voice to a constant and very human state:

> My soul was a burden, bruised and bleeding. It was tired of the man who carried it, but I found no place to set it down to rest. Neither the charm of the countryside nor the sweet scents of a garden could soothe it. It found no peace in song or laughter, none in the company of friends at table or in the pleasures of love, none even in books or poetry . . . Where could my heart find refuge from itself? Where could I go, yet leave myself behind?[4]

Augustine's reflection on the complex and conflicted nature of humanity has a lengthy pedigree, going back to the beginnings of recorded history. You may recall that in the biblical story of the first homicide,[5] Cain's punishment for killing his brother Abel is not the death penalty, which a literal reading of biblical imperatives might judge as appropriate and sanctioned. Rather, it consists of two elements. First, "The land will not yield its strength to you," which meant farming would be hard work. Second, Cain is condemned to be a ceaseless wanderer. That cannot be the whole story because four verses later, Cain settles in the land of Nod (the Hebrew word means restlessness) and marries a woman and has a child, Enoch. The text then informs us that Cain establishes a city and names the new settlement after his son.

Provocatively, the Hebrew Bible describes Cain and family as the first city dwellers, an intriguing reflection as the English word "civilization" derives from the Latin for city. In linking Cain's story with the origin of cities, the Bible reflects a judgment that violence was endemic to city living. Alas, that ancient assessment is all too relevant in our day.

How is it possible that Deity articulates a penalty that seems immediately contradicted by the text itself? In what manner can one be both a ceaseless wanderer and a city dweller? The only and obvious response is that the Bible uses stories for more than conveying facts. The biblical record has power not because it is another or even the most important history book. Rather, it succeeds (or fails) because it conveys eternal and timely truths about the human experience. Again, we need to read the Bible seriously and not literally.

Cain's punishment is our predicament. We are existential, conflicted wanderers. At the heart of our conflict is a struggle with matters of self-esteem. As Groucho Marx so wisely observed, "I wouldn't want to belong to a club that would have me as a member."[6]

That psychological complexity is embedded in us all. The sages of the Talmud[7] locate two inclinations in every person. One they label *yetzer harah*. Literally, it translates as the evil inclination. The other is the *yetzer tov*, the good inclination. But there is nuance and subtlety to these categories as suggested in the tale in which the sages imagine a moment when they personify and successfully capture the *yetzer harah*. While they debate how and whether to dispose of her,[8] they notice that no one undertakes any new enterprise; no marriages take place and "[they] looked in the whole land of Israel for a fresh egg and could not find [one]."[9]

The story wrestles with the paradox that virtue has a shadow side we call vice even as every vice may include a capacity for good. That inconvenient reality means that in the real world, despite our childlike desire for clarity and certainty, what constitutes right or wrong is often complex and confused. The evil, perhaps more accurately described as the ego inclination, has a creative and positive role in human enterprise. Selfishness may serve others as surely as complete self-sacrifice that may sometimes be the wrong course.

That complexity recalls American poet Nikki Giovanni's lines, offered during the memorial convocation for the slain of Virginia Tech: "We are better than we think, and not quite what we want to be."[10]

For some time, I have experienced that notion as an interior monologue, one that insists I am more than I ever thought I would be and less than I should be. Both statements are true. I believe it accurate to suggest that I am a wonderful father, while it is equally true that I am an incompetent parent (after all, is anyone qualified for the job?). Similarly, I would say that I am an outstanding rabbi *and* still not sufficiently qualified to offer serious teaching or counsel to all those who may request such of me. A person comes to my office with an urgent personal matter. Despite the books on my shelves and with all the years of study, I do not always have the knowledge, insight, and wisdom to respond effectively.

We all struggle with this conflict between expectations and reality. Problems inevitably arise when we only hear and only respond to one of those conflicting messages. For instance, the realization of failing to measure up as a parent often translates into disappointment or anger directed at either the child or oneself. Parents wrestling with their own failures and shortcomings, I believe, are the origin of much child abuse. Our distress must come out. Often that means verbal or physical violence of the child. Or if the parent is the focal point for those feelings of inadequacy and rage, a likely result is depression, the classic definition of which is anger turned inward.

We are all more than we thought and less than we should be. Or, as American philosopher and writer Ralph Waldo Emerson expressed, "God never made anything that didn't have a crack in it."[11]

Growth of self and connection to others are dependent upon acceptance of our dual and flawed nature. To take liberties with a cliché of transactional analysis, I'm not okay and you're not okay either. But that's okay. For if the only way in which we may be acceptable to ourselves and others is by being complete, whole, or perfect, we are all doomed. Hence, the wisdom of Dr. Carl Rogers: "The curious paradox is when I accept myself just as I am, then I can change."[12]

Roger's insight returns us to the focal point of our journey. If we are to embrace fully the miracles around and in us, we must acknowledge that we are distracted and conflicted. We must accept that the greatest barriers lie within us. That recognition leads us to the challenge and the work to which we now turn.

FOR FURTHER REFLECTION:

1. Can you identify the elements that distract you from the pursuit of spiritual growth?
2. What strategies are available to make those distractions less intrusive?
3. What elements in your character may interfere with spiritual growth?

CHAPTER 5

In Praise of Reframing

Reframing experience can remove the barriers that prevent us from seeing the miracles that sustain a rich, spiritual life.

HOW DO WE DO the work that will lead to a more fulsome embrace of life? Any journey for self-growth or mindfulness includes obstacles and distractions, not the least of these being the routines and responsibilities of daily life. Then, too, personal growth is a risky business. Many people, despite Socrates warning, find the "unexamined life"[1] to be a perfectly acceptable refuge.[2] For others, the response is obvious, even built into our essence: we act upon the conviction that we are here to grow in awareness and in character. To do otherwise would be to squander the gift of life.

Again, the Hebrew Bible addresses these issues. Consider a statement found in the Ten Commandments, one that seems to suggest a payoff for living in accord with the divine command to honor parents, namely, "Your days will be long upon the land."[3]

At first hearing, the verse seems to indicate that appropriate conduct results in a long life. But anyone of modest life experience knows that this sentiment, however much desired, isn't true. Good people too frequently suffer indignities and attenuated lives, while persons we rightly judge as deficient in character enjoy a host of undeserved benefits. The notion that length of years accrues to those who obey divine imperatives cannot be the last word.

But with reflection, the verse yields a different and more essential meaning. "Your days will be long" does not promise life extension as a reward. Rather, it intends that by living in accord with a specific discipline, our days, however many may be assigned to us, will be fuller and our time enriched. This means we may become more aware of and alive to our lives. Such is echoed in the classic toast: "May you live all the days of your life."[4] While that statement is rarely fulfilled, it is possible to provide, if not guarantee, opportunities to seize life and get more out of life as we put more of ourselves into it.

I learned this most profoundly as a consequence of my father's death or, more precisely, from his dying. I was a teenager when my dad received a terminal cancer prognosis. The doctors gave him no more than six months, although he survived for two and a half years. From such news, one might imagine his son concluding that life cannot be trusted. More specifically, it isn't worth the pain. After all, to live means we outlive, and to love means we lose. Who wants or needs that?

My father, however, shared a different vision. Conveyed in four lessons, I consider them the most important things I know.

The first is obvious, if often ignored. All life is a gift, a very precious and fragile one.

That means (lesson number two) that were I to die today, I want more. I am intoxicated just by being alive. I wish to hold my life and those who are part of it tightly, such that I might never, were it in my power, let it or them go. As Emily Dickinson reminds us, "To live is so startling, it leaves but little room for other occupations."[5]

Then comes lesson number three. Were I to die today, it would be enough to say the gift of life was worth it. I still want more, but if this shall be my portion, it would be sufficient to say, "Thank you."

Finally, lesson four, I would rather have my father than have learned any of the above. I cannot have that, but I can hold fast to what his life continues to mean for me. I admit there are days when his death, now so many years ago, feels present and painful. But there are many more days when I give thanks that he is part of me even as I continue to wish he were not apart from me.

Dad was the first person to point out to me that people fall into two categories. Some seem predisposed to complain. No matter what the circumstance, their response is negative, always some variation of "why poor me?" They may endure little more than a metaphorical hangnail, yet they conclude, not unlike the only recently freed and endlessly complaining Hebrews of the Exodus drama, that the whole world has conspired to afflict them. Meanwhile, other people endure a cascading series of indignities, illness or injury, and despite those circumstances continue to embrace life with a steady conviction that, with all its vagaries and difficulties, the journey is the prize.

How do we understand or explain those different responses to life experiences? Some people possess resources to continue in the face of calamity while others express only pain and despair at the mildest of setbacks. Is it nature or nurture, or randomness? I don't know the answer, but I vividly recall an occasion that brought the dichotomy into high relief.

The setting was a pastoral visit to a hospital. How long ago will be clear in the telling. I received a call from the hospital chaplain that a patient wanted to see a rabbi. I dutifully made my way to the hospital. As soon as I entered the room, I recalled French fashion designer Coco Chanel's warning that "by the time you're fifty, you get the face you deserve."[6] Had this hospitalized lady been a book, I would never have gotten past the cover. Not that she was ugly or handsome; it was more an immediate awareness that her face seemed marinated in rage. And, indeed, she was angry on my arrival. She had been hospitalized because of a severely broken leg and arm (injuries that would almost certainly not require hospitalization today). The targets for her anger were numerous, including the doctors who could not heal her according to her demanding standards and schedule. She was angry with the nurses for tending to more seriously ill patients. She was angry with God for providing a world that included ice, an unfortunate encounter with which caused her hospitalization. As well, I remember, she was angry with me. My offense was nothing more than to walk into her room, even though I presumably was responding to her request, or at least I thought so. The only assistance, if any, I provided was to serve as another target for her expressions of displeasure.

Since I was already at the hospital, I stopped in to visit another patient. This woman, paralyzed from the neck down, smiled at me. I'll never forget that smile, the teaching she imparted, and the healing that came with it. Whence that audacity? Fate had dealt her terrible cards, self-evidently more distressing and severe than the lady with broken body parts. Nonetheless, this person knew that she still could shape some part of her destiny by how she played her hand. So she continued to connect with beauty, caring, and uplift. She embraced the conviction that life, with all its challenges and limitations, was worth it. She made an unforgettable difference in my life and, not surprisingly, many others.

That evening, I happened upon a story. Two children are playing in a garden. The first child comes home and declares, "Mommy, what a cruel place the garden is. All the rose bushes have thorns on them." The other child rushes in to exclaim, "Mommy, what a beautiful place the garden is. All the thorn bushes have roses on them."[7] More than a clever reframing, the story captures that fundamental tension in our lives.

Perhaps you share with me the experience of your parents promising you a garden filled with roses. "We just want you to be happy" is one of the more common expressions of this sentiment. It translates as, you should have a contented and carefree life. The only problem, and a rather substantial one, is that life includes no shortage of thorns. Must we inevitably injure ourselves on the thorns? And in such circumstances, how might we take note of the roses?

The roses are always there. Annie Dillard, the author of *Pilgrim at Tinker Creek*[8] and so many other remarkable explorations of our humanity, writes that were we genuinely present in a moment, in every or at least more moments, the experience would compare to an attempt to fill a wine cup under a waterfall. It would be overwhelming. We may either lament the loss of so much experience or embrace the conviction that there is always more to imbibe, always an opportunity to toast and celebrate the blessing that resides in all things. That may even include the disappointment and pain that come to us. As the Sufi poet, Rumi, instructs in *The Guest House*:

> This being human is a guest house.
> Every morning a new arrival.
>
> A joy, a depression, a meanness,
> some momentary awareness comes
> as an unexpected visitor.
>
> Welcome and entertain them all!
> Even if they're a crowd of sorrows,
> who violently sweep your house
> empty of its furniture,
> still, treat each guest honorably.
> He may be clearing you out
> for some new delight.
>
> The dark thought, the shame, the malice,
> meet them at the door laughing,
> and invite them in.
>
> Be grateful for whoever comes,
> because each has been sent
> as a guide from beyond.[9]

The key is never what happens. It is how we respond to our experience. "Circumstances and situations do color life," writes Robert Holden, "but you have been given the mind to choose what the color shall be."[10]

This is key to taking miracles seriously and to appreciating what Moses may teach us from the mountaintop even if we dwell too regularly in a valley of somnolence. Miracles are ever present in our world. We only need to reframe the distractions and clutter of everyday life to recognize that the commonplace is a path full of wonder and miracle. In that awareness, we find the colors to transform mere living into a genuine masterpiece of and for life.

FOR FURTHER REFLECTION:

1. Are you able to identify strategies that make it possible for you to live, if not all, then more of the days of your life?
2. What concrete steps can you take now to reach that goal?

PART 2

Taking God Seriously

I T IS IMPOSSIBLE TO examine what we mean by holiness or the
sacred, at least for Western spirituality, without an exploration of
what one may assert about God, be that at the heart of our life
pursuit or a concept devoid of any serious meaning to us, and all the
possible variations between those extremes. Whatever one's point of view,
including uncertainty, doubt, frustration, fear, or confusion, the chapters
here insist that some respect for, or a nod toward, the wisdom of antiquity
requires an examination of what we mean by the divine and what an
intellectually defensible position about God may add to our connection
to the miracles all around us and in us.

CHAPTER 6

Some Fun before We Plunge

We don't need to be only serious when we explore serious ideas about God.

S OME READERS JUDGE ANY discussion of God as problematic, obscure, or even esoteric, a conclusion I hope to avoid. It perhaps helps to begin the encounter with a lighter touch.

The late Broadway titan Moss Hart[1] was especially proud of a major landscaping project accomplished at enormous personal expense at his country home in Bucks County, Pennsylvania. Once, while showing it off to friends, either S. J. Perelman or Dorothy Parker (sources differ) responded: "Gee, Moss, imagine what God could do if He had your money." [2]

Hart's story recalls another tale of a country minister's visit to the farm of a congregant. The proud farmer delights in showing the preacher his superbly maintained fields. The minister can't restrain his enthusiasm and, consistent with his calling, couches his praise in theological terms. "You know," he says, "it's remarkable what God and you have done with this place." The farmer's immediate reply, "Reverend, you should have seen what a mess it was when only God ran it."

It is noteworthy that the farmer asserts we are not meant to be mere passive recipients of divine largess. Rather, we have a role to play. In fact, Jewish tradition, with remarkable *chutzpah*,[3] insists that humanity and Deity are in partnership. While that may sound disquieting or even absurd to some, those who embrace the concept recognize that, at most, we are very junior partners in the arrangement.

Every Western religious tradition insists that humanity needs Deity. But this "family business" embraces the radical elaboration that God also needs humanity in order to make a better world. The more skeptical among us, especially when it comes to any positive affirmation about God, may consider the latter idea as a high-blown or desperate effort to attach transcendent value to human endeavor. But I take the contention with utmost seriousness. Be it true or fantasy, it provides purpose and focus to life.

Readers by now have heard that I argue against a literalist approach to religious ideas. I do so, especially, in discussions on ideas about God, a subject fraught with difficulties, not the least of which is the heavy presence of so many literalists who embrace a univocal position as if it were the only authentic and possible response. Some of those are defenders of religion. Others are found among the increasing number of militants and, I would say, equally fundamentalist atheists. The two camps have much in common. Each insists that what we mean by the word "God" be limited to one narrow interpretation with all other options ruled out of order.

That recalls an occasion when I was visiting the home of a congregant to pay a sympathy call. While we conversed in their living room, my eye took in the coffee table upon which I noticed a magazine with a scantily clad woman on the cover. I also observed a headline near the top of that cover: "Isaac Asimov: "Do Scientists Believe in God?" The topic was of obvious importance to me as a rabbi. I also happen to be a science fiction fan, especially the works of Asimov. What to do? With some trepidation, I decided to seek permission to pick up the magazine. After all, it was in plain view. Going to considerable lengths to explain my dispassionate and solely "academic interest" in that one headline, I asked if I might take a look. With permission, I turned the pages to the article. As I recall, Asimov's comments went something like this:

> The Bible says the world was created in six days. Six means six. In fact, it is the only thing it can mean, which is, of course, absolute nonsense. So, anyone who takes the Bible seriously is, then, a fool.

I was upset by that suggestion. I take the Bible very seriously, but I don't think the world literally came to be in six days. Further, I consider myself far more a *seeker* than a fool. I contemplated writing a letter to the editor but then thought better of the idea, not keen to have my name in the magazine (although who would ever admit seeing my letter in those pages?).

Both defenders of religion and a substantial number of its critics would agree with Asimov's assertion. Six has only one narrow and precise meaning. So they exchange calumny, both agreeing in the literalism, one side embracing it, the other ridiculing it. Obviously, I do not espouse either position, although I'm aware that my position does not suffer for lack of challenges. With that in mind, let's embark on that discussion.

FOR FURTHER REFLECTION:

1. Assuming we are in partnership with God, how might you more effectively demonstrate your value to that partnership?

CHAPTER 7

Finding a Sacred Dimension
in All of Us

The Hebrew Bible offers a profound idea and ideal about the connection between holiness and humanity.

WONDER AND MIRACLE ARE all around us and in us, and, wonderfully, wondrously, we can experience that sacred context. Skeptics might say, "You must be kidding" or, perhaps a bit kinder, "So what?" I prefer Gerard Manley Hopkins' insistence that there is but one conclusion, namely "The world is charged with the grandeur of God."[1] Don't let Hopkins' traditionally religious language obscure the insight. There is abundant evidence of holiness all around us. "The fullness of the whole earth is God's presence," said the biblical prophet Isaiah.[2]

Nonetheless, I know an increasing number of people are, at best, uncomfortable with *God talk*, but if you've come this far, I implore you to suspend disbelief. I promise to address that challenge later on; it is not unfamiliar refrain, and it deserves attention.

Irving Howe, a much-admired scholar and an avowed atheist of a previous generation, once said to me, "You seem like an intelligent person. Why in the world do you take God and religion seriously?"

With deference to Howe and others, I offer a compromise. One may interpret Isaiah's statement as insisting that the whole earth points to a sacred or hallowed presence. That awareness does not require, at least not yet, that there be any person or personality labeled Deity. Nonetheless, logic suggests that if there be an exalted dimension around us, then it must extend to us and in us. By which I mean, even with its old religious tones, Motel the Tailor of *Fiddler on the Roof* [3] fame has a point:

> But of all God's miracles, large and small,
> The most miraculous one of all,
> Is that out of a worthless lump of clay,
> God has made a man today.

One does not have to take literally the lyric to find significance in it. No defiance of science is required to acknowledge that "what lies behind us and what lies before us are small matters compared to what lies within us."[4] And yet our response to that reflection need not conform to any scientific theory in order to convey a sublime value.

Whether one has an abiding confidence in God's presence or believes God is an hypothesis for which there is no convincing evidence, the creation story in Genesis provides a remarkable and a unique point of view on who and what humans are. One need not judge the story of the world's creation in seven days as fact to find transcendent value in it. I use the word "transcendent" intentionally. It is my conviction that the Hebrew Bible employs the story form not to convey facts but to express values. Again, the tale need not be true to convey an important truth.

The Bible's creation account provides an awesome notion about human beings. It intends to apply to everyone, not just to one distinct tribe or community or gender. Rather, the description embraces all of us; as the text insists, we are created in the "image of God."[5] And while familiarity with the phrase may lead to indifference or worse, the original Hebrew is instructive, provocative, and maybe even inspiring.

The controlling word is *"Tselem,"* which may be translated as image. But in its most common usage, *Tselem* is a synonym for an idol. Anyone with a passing familiarity with the Hebrew Bible's focus will recognize that iconoclasm, in the classic sense of smashing idols, is prominent throughout. In fact, the biblical tradition appears more obsessed with battling *against* idolatry than advocating *for* God.

Yet that same contentious word, *Tselem*, gets applied to us. The only time the word is used positively is in describing humanity and that cannot be without import or intent. The phrase *image of God* defines or describes what the text claims as the divine perspective on humanity's value, consequence, and responsibility. Put another way, the Hebrew Bible might be understood better as a sacred anthropology than a book of theology.

Again leaving aside factual accuracy, the essential question is, what does it mean if human beings are created in the image of God? What would it require if we acknowledge that every person is infused with some majestic, sacred stuff—that each of us is of infinite value, a subject rather than an object, a person and not a thing?

In its own time, and even now, the biblical view is nothing less than revolutionary. That is the meaning found in a commentary that begins with the question, "What is the greatest sin a person can commit?" After all the attempts, including monstrous acts like murder and adultery, the commentary insists the greatest sin is to forget our pedigree, our ancestry, that we are children of royalty.[6]

Consider, by contrast, one of humanity's oldest stories. Called the *Enuma Elish*, it is the creation myth of ancient Mesopotamia. Briefly summarized, it describes a multitude of gods engaged in ceaseless warfare which they determine must be resolved. The two sides pick their champion, who will fight to the death. Interestingly, gods can die in this telling. The good gods, that is, the ones who will win, choose as their defender Marduk.[7] The bad gods (the losers) choose as their combatant Tiamat. And here the myth becomes especially noteworthy. The name *Tiamat* translates as chaos. She is a goddess whose form is a serpent.

We may conclude, assuredly, that men wrote this story. The description of Tiamat conveys all the male ambivalence toward the female. She is goddess and, simultaneously, the embodiment of chaos. So, with an all too clear conscience and with our masculine turmoil on display, we blame her for our confusion.

Interestingly, Tiamat's form as a snake evokes a parallel to the serpent in the Garden of Eden.[8] In Genesis, the snake brings chaos into the narrative. But more commonly in the ancient world, a snake is a symbol of rejuvenation and renewal, even of eternal life. That conviction still echoes in the Rod of Asclepius, the ancient and still common emblem of the healing arts, which pictures a snake curled around a staff.[9] Could the staff represent a tree or *the* tree of life?

Marduk and Tiamat meet in single combat, from which Marduk emerges victorious. In his triumph, he cuts up Tiamat's body, the parts of which provide the raw material from which, inadvertently, the world emerges. That is no small matter, for if accidental, the inescapable conclusion is that life has no meaning or purpose. For the world may be full of sound and fury, but it signifies nothing more than an unintended consequence of Marduk's victorious frenzy.

Even more telling is the origin of humanity. When I speak in public about this story, I often ask the audience to guess which of Tiamat's body parts gave rise to us. The point of the exercise isn't to come up with the right answer. Rather, the audience suggestions invariably reflect a point of view about our essence or nature. Someone will offer the stomach as a metaphor for our appetites, our always wanting more. Another frequent guess is the tongue as a symbol for the human capacity for speech. The heart is mentioned, too, as the repository of our feelings and emotive nature.[10] And while those responses tend to reflect a relatively positive view of humanity's value, they are miles removed from the Mesopotamian story. In this tale, we are the by-product of the contents of the goddess' entrails. We are not even fully formed feces; we are worthless and, more likely, offensive.

One does not need to imagine that the *Enuma Elish* represents an accurate account of how the world or humanity came to be in order to appreciate that the myth reflects and shapes a worldview. The biblical and Mesopotamian accounts are among the earliest representations of a clash of opposites. Is life a matter of design and purpose or mere accident?

Both the biblical creation story and the *Enuma Elish* are myths, which should not be confused with falsehoods or fairy tales. Myths provided the ancients with a symbolic language or road map that conveyed and shaped a specific notion of the world and our place in it. They continue to provide a remarkable window into cultures and human values. At the least, myths are humanity's ancient, timeless way of expressing specific, subjective, and/or illusory convictions, even when idiosyncratically linked to one specific group. There is no easy escape from them, for we live as much in our interpretation of a place as in the place itself. In demythologized terms, the *Enuma Elish* and the Genesis account provide stark contrast, not only with details about character and plot but most of all in their fundamental assertion. One insists that life is an accident; the other, that life is flush with purpose and design.

It is the height of naivete not to recognize that myths provide a critical framework for our world. Prince Charming and Snow White not only impact the imaginations of the young but also imbue many with the dreamlike conviction that there has to be one perfect someone whose magical embrace will transform our drab circumstances into a happily-ever-after perfection. And mythic constructs are not limited to an earlier time or to moments of child-like naivete. Consider all that is implicitly conveyed in advertisements trying to convince us that the right automobile, preferably a sports car, will transform a drab existence into a saga of adventure. Hugh Hefner of *Playboy* fame (or ignominy) made a fortune to fuel his sybaritic life by selling a myth or vision of the girl next door as perpetually virginal and sexually available. Similarly entangled in fantasy, just about every superhero movie is a variation of the lone gunslinger cleaning up the town. These and other notions shape and often distort our view of how our lives are supposed to be.

In its own time, and I would argue for our time as well, the Bible offers a genuinely strange, original story. Creation is orderly with logic and intent. At the last moment of the final day, we learn that human beings are fashioned with image of God *in* them. The story expresses a value, one worlds removed from the conviction that human beings are little more than (with apologies) crap.

What, then, might it mean if human beings are the image of God? The phrase indicates that we may experience a sacred dimension, not only in ineffable moments like a star-filled sky or a single tear but also, and maybe especially, in the person near you. The wonderful storyteller Harry Golden[11] recalled, "When I was young, I asked my father, 'If you don't believe in God, why do you go to synagogue so regularly?' His father answered, 'Jews go to synagogue for all sorts of reasons. My friend Garfinkel, who is pious, goes to talk with God. I go to talk with Garfinkel.'"

The Hebrew Bible insists that when you are really meeting with, talking to, caring about any and every Garfinkel, you are getting as close as possible to a genuine experience of God. That must be why the same Hebrew word translated as image (*Tselem*) is the root for the modern Hebrew verb to take a photograph. If you'd like to see an image of God, take a look at the person next to you and take a close look at yourself. This is the point of a marvelous rabbinic legend, which tells us that every human being is accompanied by a retinue of angels. With shofars[12] blasting, they call out, "Make way for the image of God. Make way for the image of God."

Unlike the Greek philosopher Xenophanes' famous nostrum—if the donkeys had a Deity, it would look like a donkey, including long ears and tail—I do not propose that humanity as the image of God is literally true. God does not look like us or the reverse. But our lifelong task is to transform the concept into a lived reality, to embrace the ultimate value in all of us. We do that work in the way we connect with others and in the way we imagine or, more precisely, image ourselves.

A little girl turns to her mother. "Mommy, the rabbi's sermon confused me."

The mother replies, "Oh, why is that?"

The child answers, "Well, he said that God is bigger than we are. Is that true, Mommy?"

"Yes, that's true, honey."

"But, Mommy, he also said that a part of God lives in us. Is that true?"

Again, the mother replies, "Yes."

"Well," said the little girl, "if God is bigger than us and lives in us, wouldn't God show through?"[13]

Among the challenges of the biblical telling is that you and I are supposed to be full of God. We should be a place where, as the girl suggests, God shows through. And our primary way of demonstrating, of serving, of meeting Deity is in our relations with each other. Rabbi Akiba, a second-century sage and martyr, makes a bold declaration: "Great love was shown to humankind in that we are created in the divine image, even greater love that we can know that we are created in the divine image."[14] His words are echoed in the lyric from *Les Misérables:* "To love another person is to see the face of God."

The biblical conviction asserts that no matter what we do for a living, our true profession is to be reminders of God. Doing so would have a transformative, even miraculous effect, certainly for ourselves, if not on our world.

Some may hear that as little more than a variation of secular humanism masquerading in religious garb. But for Hebrew Scripture, secular humanism is impossible. Positively stated, to be in the image of God means there is only the sacred—the miraculous that is all around us and in us. The blind and deaf Helen Keller embraced that wisdom: "I believe that God is in me as the sun is in the color and fragrance of a flower; the Light in my darkness, the Voice in my silence."[15]

From my perspective, it is possible and preferable to live with that conviction, that intensity, especially because when you've met one image of God, you haven't exhausted the opportunities as you cannot meet them all. Each encounter has the potential to become a moment when Isaiah's fullness of the earth and human experience come together. Each can testify that the journey of life contains incalculable vitality and value.

FOR FURTHER REFLECTION:

1. What value may be added to our lives if we imagine that every person possesses a sacred quality?
2. What role, if any, do myths play in your life?
3. Can you recall persons or times when the enthusiasm of an encounter led you to experience overwhelming or transcendent joy?
4. If so, how might that encounter have changed you and how may you keep that memory as an active part of the times that follow thereafter?

CHAPTER 8

Swimming in a Sea
of Uncertainty

We can move forward with God, even without certainty, in the modern world.

WITH THE NOTABLE EXCEPTION of science fiction, we live only in our specific moment, which means we bring with us—we cannot do otherwise—all the perspective and/or prejudice of that precise moment in time. And while there are those who argue that ours is a postmodern and post-faith age, I begin this exploration with an effort to understand what is meant by modernity and its aftermath, which in the world of ideas leads directly to René Descartes.

Often called the father of modern philosophy, Descartes lived in a world in which a certainty about absolute truths was giving way to an absolute of uncertainty. Centuries-old and unquestioned truths, including belief in the historical accuracy of the Bible, were yielding to new insights from science. Old moorings were losing their hold; ambiguity and doubt were gaining currency. Thinkers sought to manage the destabilizing rush of scientific discovery by presenting science as the path to a renewed and stable world order. But science would not sit still. The new scientific order would need to be constantly revised, modified, or reversed as new data and new facts confounded what had only recently been embraced as stable and true.

The revisions are still going on, centuries after Descartes, as this anecdote from the *Wall Street Journal* confirms:

> One of my professors in graduate school . . . delivered a lecture on a Tuesday about a topic in ecology, only to read a paper the next day that invalidated what he had just taught. So he went into his class on Thursday and said: "Remember what I told you on Tuesday? It's wrong. And if that worries you, you need to get out of science."[1]

Descartes' base question, one that haunts us still, is "Of what may I be sure?" His only recourse was to construct his philosophy on a foundation of doubt. Beginning with his assumption of an *I* who cannot be sure, he famously stated, *cogito ergo sum*, "I think; therefore, I am." That familiar phrase might equally, even more precisely, be expressed as "I doubt; therefore, I am." In the context of the world of ideas, so begin the modern age and its consequences for the human condition.

For some, pervasive uncertainty fuels a hunger for orthodox convictions. It results in a sometimes desperate attempt to escape doubt, as though its presence undermines our ability to achieve any notion of a meaningful existence. At the least, starting with the self, a hallmark of our age, leads to solipsism or, in philosophical terms, an end to objective truth. Continuing a lengthy philosophical argument, Bertrand Russell asked how we could even prove there is an external world. His default response was that we couldn't: "It must be admitted that we can never prove the existence of things other than ourselves."[2] The Chinese philosopher Chuang Tzu expresses the challenge more evocatively: "Last night I dreamt I was a golden butterfly. Am I a man who dreamt he was a golden butterfly, or am I now a golden butterfly dreaming he is a man?"[3]

How, then, can we be certain, in this day and age, of the existence of God? As one clever commentator suggests, it is as impossible for a person to demonstrate the existence of God as it is for Sherlock Holmes to demonstrate the existence of Arthur Conan Doyle.[4] Yet I believe there are signposts amid the uncertainty, matters that point to more than themselves, and perhaps more than we can say.

Consider the folktale about twins in the womb.[5] One of the twins believes there is life after the womb: "Not only is there life after the womb, but also, after we leave, we'll breathe air." The other twin, a skeptic, insists there is nothing after the womb: "You're crazy. Everyone knows life is only possible in water."

The believing twin continues: "Not only will we breathe air, but we'll also eat through the mouth." This enrages the skeptic: "It's a well-known scientific fact that all nourishment comes through the umbilical cord."

As they continue to argue, the twins are interrupted by an earthquake. More precisely, labor begins. As fortune (and good storytelling) would have it, the believing twin descends the birth canal first. The skeptic sees an explosion of light and hears a cry, which leads to the conclusion: "It's worse than I thought. It's not that there is no life after the womb. There is punishment after the womb."

While many see a great division between those who call themselves religious and those who embrace some variation of a scientific, secular, or anti-religious position, the twin story reflects one of my core convictions. I believe every human being is religious. In effect, the twins' differing views of reality represent what religion means, not in the narrow sense of observing particular rituals, attending houses of worship, and affirming specific doctrine, but more broadly. I argue that there are only two fundamental religious positions. One asserts that life is precious and meaningful; the other insists, with equal conviction, that life is meaningless. Everything else, including custom, costume, and creed, is elaboration from either starting point. Remarkable to me, the latter position has legions of adherents, among them philosopher Thomas Carlyle, who once famously called our world "a hall of doom." I am also aware that some who believe life is meaningful find no need or room for God in their understanding of what it means to be human.[6]

Our choice between those two fundamental positions—our choice of ultimate values—will determine who and what we are and what we shall become. Ralph Waldo Emerson puts it this way:

> The gods we worship write their names on our faces, be sure of that. And we will worship something—have no doubt of that either. We may think that our tribute is paid in secret in the dark recesses of the heart—but it will out. That which dominates our imagination and our thoughts will determine our life and character. Therefore, it behooves us to be careful what we are worshiping, for what we are worshiping we are becoming.[7]

I am far from alone in my conclusion that the principal religion of the United States is not one of the streams of Christianity but materialism, the sure conviction that salvation, at least happiness and fulfillment, comes from *things*, especially if those items convey the right image or brand. We just need more stuff, the right stuff. All that is necessary to attend "church" is to turn on television, computer, or smartphone; the worship begins as a cascade of images convey the essential credo that money is the quick and easy solution to every problem.

Like every other form of idolatry, the worship of money inevitably leads to human sacrifice, whether writ large in the human toll of lives wasted in pursuit of maximizing profits and share prices or more intimately in the form of family connections lost in service to time at the office.

Again, the issue isn't God or no God, for everyone holds a set of essential convictions. We all worship, or express what we accept, consciously or not, as our ultimate reality.

The heart of the matter, then, becomes where, if anywhere, we find meaning in the experience we call life. One option, given the inescapable presence of uncertainty, is metaphorically to throw in the towel since no amount of reflection about faith in Deity will remove doubt entirely. Alternatively, the lengthy and centuries-long list of persons who have provided us with writings and arguments about finding meaning through a connection to God provides strong evidence that serious reflections about God are possible and worthwhile. Uncertainty is real, but that does not mean that seeking a connection to the sacred is irrational or folly.

FOR FURTHER REFLECTION:

1. I assert in this chapter that all people, even those who claim to the contrary, are religious. What do you identify as the core elements of your religion?
2. What are your essential or ultimate values?
3. Are there elements in your life that may fall into the category of idol worship?

CHAPTER 9

The Child's Complaint, "That's Not Fair"

The biblical Book of Job is a startling encounter with the capriciousness of life, and the impact of suffering on our belief in and relationship with God.

M OST OF US GROW up with a theology that resembles a variation on the Santa Claus motif.[1]

You better watch out,
You better not cry,
Better not pout,
I'm telling you why:
Santa Claus is comin' to town.

He's making a list
And checking it twice,
Gonna find out
Who's naughty and nice.
Santa Claus is comin' to town.

He sees you when you're sleepin',
He knows when you're awake,
he knows if you've been bad or good,
So be good for goodness sake . . .

Just substitute God for the St. Nick references, and you have a major obstacle to an intelligent consideration of Deity, namely a system with an unerring CEO who rewards the good and, of course, punishes those who fail to meet a demanding standard. Yet it would be remarkable if what a child may believe about the world were to serve an adult equally well, unchallenged and unchanged.

Nonetheless, the song provides an opportunity for reflection. Beyond any moment of sadness or anger when the child discovers Santa isn't real, the last line is especially interesting. "So be good for goodness sake" may be understood as no more than an expletive. Come on! Wise up! Behave! Or, as I prefer, it may be heard another way, as a secret teaching and the only honest line in the song.

We all know fine people who suffer indignities and others who embrace a range of ugly behaviors yet still seem to accumulate every advantage. Which leads to the question, why do good things happen to bad people?

More personally, even if intended ironically, there are moments when I wonder what it would be like not to be stuck with a strong sense of ethics and values. I imagine getting away with a variety of illicit and profitable activities, save that I'd have to live with myself.

That reflection brings to mind a meeting with Nelson Mandela. To describe him as a giant is an understatement. Nearly twenty-eight years of his life was stolen by a corrupt apartheid regime, yet he had no interest or time for anger or revenge. How is it possible to explain his restraint and composure?

I was privileged to hear Mandela refer to the South African tribal concept *seriti*. Although not easily translated into an equivalent English word, some suggest it means dignity or integrity. The Sotho[2] get closer to Mandela's intention, however, by referring to *seriti* as "the shadow that you cast."

Seriti embodies a conviction that while the life force resides in me, I should recognize myself as a finite, yet precious custodian of an unlimited resource. Should I spend my time in anger, even when the other may deserve it, or in settling scores, even with full justification for it, I likely would become a person with whom I'd hope to be uncomfortable. *Seriti* insists that how I treat others is independent of their treatment of me. Whether or not they have earned or deserve some kindness, I will be compassionate. *Seriti* is a remarkable and renewable resource insisting that our lifelong focus is to grow in quality, character, or soul.

That effort offers no guarantee or promise to change the circumstances of my life, be they fine or painful. The only benefit is how I respond to my situation. Not surprisingly, the Hebrew Bible includes an extraordinary account that expands on this theme.

Both in form and content, the Book of Job[3] is a strong candidate for the most important, difficult, and misunderstood volume in the Bible. It has three distinct sections: a brief prose opening, a substantial and very challenging body in poetry, and a terse prose conclusion.

The story begins with our learning that Job's suffering is a test or, worse, the result of a bragging contest between God and HaSatan.[4] Essentially, we find God in the heavenly court pontificating, one might say, about how wonderful Job is. HaSatan's rejoinder: "Great guy, he's had all the breaks, money, family, prestige, the best clubs. Everything's going his way. Why wouldn't he think life is grand?"

Were we not conditioned to assign profundity to pronouncements in the Bible, we would miss the outrageous, even ugly nature of what follows. The text indicates God takes the bait. Job is left in HaSatan's power with one stipulation: "You just can't touch him." A series of calamities follow, including total financial ruin and the catastrophic death of Job's children. King Lear comes to mind: "As flies to wanton boys are we to th' gods.

They kill us for their sport."[5] Yet Job refuses to concede to sin or absurdity. He remains faithful.

With that, we return to the court on high, where God is at it again. "Adversary, you stirred me against that great fellow Job, but he came through. What a guy!" To use the text itself, the adversary parries: "Lay a hand on his bones and his flesh, and he will surely blaspheme You to Your face."[6] Deity goes along. Job suffers some loathsome and painful affliction. Old translations call it leprosy; newer ones, a "severe inflammation from the sole of his foot to the crown of his head."[7] As a result, we find Job quarantined to a dung heap or, in more refined versions, a pile of ashes. His wife urges him to curse God and die, but not our Job, who replies, "Should we accept only good . . . and not accept evil?"

Three friends show up. They say not a word for seven days, which is either the last good thing they do or the most they can offer.

With that, the text switches to poetry, the vast majority of which may be described, albeit insufficiently, as an argument between Job and his previously silent comforters, as they defend their presumption that Job must have done something wrong. A just God does justly; therefore, you must deserve these chastisements, to which Job dissents. In precis, he insists, "I did not sin, and even were that so, I do not deserve what has befallen me." His interlocutors think Job's declaration of innocence convicts him of overwhelming pride. But Job is right. He does not deserve the sufferings that have come upon him.

An important shift follows, as Job calls God to account or at least asks Deity to defend him. And remarkably, except for the fact that we are dealing with the Bible, God shows up. In one of the most extraordinary images in any literature, Job encounters a presence, a voice speaking out of a tempest or whirlwind. While Job receives no answers for why he suffers, he is overwhelmed by an awesome mystery and with the grandeur of this experience. Critically, at the end of the poetry, Job's situation remains unchanged. He is still an everyman, positioned on a pile of ash; however, he embraces the conviction that meaning abides. Using more traditionally religious language, the text reads:

I had heard You with my ears,
But now I see You with my eyes;
Therefore, I recant and relent,
Being but dust and ashes.[8]

Immediately, the book reverts to a prose conclusion. In a very few lines, Job gets his health and positions restored. He becomes rich again, and the text informs us Job gets new children to replace those who died chapters earlier. Yet one thing is sure. The genius who conveys this story to our care knew full well that new children do not replace lost ones. That ache never goes away completely.

While we cannot explain in tidy formulas why the righteous may suffer, let alone why others who are wicked prosper, that does not mean emptiness lies at the heart of existence. In effect, Job learns that tragic and meaningless are not synonyms. And this perspective contrasts vividly, ludicrously, with a tagged-on happily-ever-after prose conclusion that is intended to subvert or cloak the truth, which, being good "for its own sake," is the only reliable and certain outcome.

There are times, more and more moments, when I, like Job, have confidence that saying *God is* means something essential. However, since I take my experience seriously, there are occasions when I'm not sure what, if anything, particular names or words indicate in reference to Deity. A critic might interject that this represents no problem, as those words lack any referent, let alone meaning. Yet I find it remarkable that in a world with uncertainty, with epistemological doubt at its core, anyone can be sure in the assertion that there is nothing, no thing to which the word "God" refers. While there are God concepts about which I am an atheist, an absolute or orthodox commitment to that position requires more confidence, more faith than I have.

Job opens the door to questioning traditional notions of an omnipotent and benevolent Deity and to the prospect that there is no meaningful referent that stands behind any God concept whatsoever. Many individuals, then, consider atheism as the only proper outcome. While I obviously disagree with the conclusion, here are three admittedly paradoxical or ironic stories in praise of atheism.

Story one. A skeptic intends to taunt a rabbi: "Rabbi, I don't believe in God. I am an atheist," he proudly declares.

The rabbi inquires, "Have you read Marx, Russell, Feuerbach, Camus, Sartre?"

"No, none of those," the skeptic replies. "Well, then, you're not an atheist. You're an ignoramus."

Story two. A student announces that he is deeply troubled by the condition of our world. So much chaos leads him to conclude there is no God. The master asks him to explain, and the student offers a litany of woes that concludes with "Just look at it. Danger and trouble are everywhere. I could have done better myself."

"Ah, my child," replies the master, "that is exactly why God put you here. Now get to work."

Story three. "Rabbi, you taught us everything has a purpose."

"Yes," replies the rabbi.

"What possible purpose could there be in God permitting atheism?"

"Oh, that's simple. When you see someone in need, at that point, you must become an atheist. Don't you dare suggest that God should help that person. You do it. You help."

Certainly there are difficulties with and doubts about God, even for clergy. People ask me, "Rabbi, do you believe in God?" My response is usually yes. Most days, I am confident about God's presence. I am convinced that it means something essential, vital, to declare God *is*. Meaning abides. Life makes sense. Yet God's purposes readily and regularly elude me. Like so many others, I am not free of doubts and perplexities. There are moments when too much mystery, pain, or tragedy summons a *why* for which neither hypothesis about God nor response from God seems persuasive or meaningful.

But whether I'm believing or doubting in a given moment, I'm always certain of this: it takes more faith than I have to be sure there is nothing to which the word "God" may refer.

Bertrand Russell, often described as a strong advocate for atheism, suggests we have no option but to build our lives upon "the firm foundation of unyielding despair."[9] I admire Russell for his passionate commitment to social justice. From disarmament and fighting poverty to advocating for sexual freedom, he was a noted and risk-taking intellectual, even though such effort seems to push against his assertion of despair. For without some standard of conduct or values, how does one determine what action may be right or wrong?

In fact, Russell bravely and correctly identifies the problem with his atheism. Ethical subjectivism reduces all discussions about values to aesthetics, which echoes an old Latin aphorism: "In matters of taste, there can be no disputes."[10] He struggles with the lack of any extrinsic absolute: "I cannot see how to refute the arguments for the subjectivity of ethical values, but I find myself incapable of believing that all that is wrong with wanton cruelty is that I don't like it."[11] If there are no standards beyond the self, if I am the measure of everything, anything goes, and one moral path is as valid as any other. If there is no objective authority against which we may measure right or wrong, determine what to do or where we stand, then one position makes as much logical sense as any other.

Maybe that explains why, later in his career, Russell seemed willing to consider agnosticism a compelling alternative to his earlier absolute conviction that there are no absolutes.

Both Mandela's embrace of *seriti* and the Job whom we meet in "his" poetry lead us to an ineluctable conclusion. In this life, what happens to us is far less crfitical than how we respond to what happens in us. After all, our life experience is fraught with confusion and uncertainty. Rather than a Santa Claus-like reliance on fairness residing at the core of life,

I find myself more aligned with a gloss linked to the poet Robert Browning, who suggests that the religious person has moments of doubt interrupted by faith. Therefore, what I adjudge as an integrity-filled struggle allows, invites, and perhaps even necessitates reflection on our belief in and relationship with God.

FOR FURTHER REFLECTION:

1. What was your response upon discovering there was no Santa Claus, Tooth Fairy, or the equivalent? Were you angry, sad, disillusioned, or unmoved?
2. What, if any, "secret" wisdom do you wish isn't true or is too grave for a child or for the child in you to acknowledge?
3. How might the concept of *seriti* change your behavior with others?

CHAPTER 10

The Danger of Not Doubting

In a time of ambiguity, we might find value in what previous generations understood as proofs of God.

WHILE SHARING SOME OF the reflections in the previous chapter with a small group of students, I received feedback that they were impressed to hear a clergyperson openly share doubt and uncertainty about Deity. They had assumed, it seems, that having faith and/or confidence with the God idea must not permit, let alone admit, to any hesitation. The frequent assumption is that admissions of doubt in the religious enterprise are evidence of a lack of faith and disqualify such persons as legitimate members of the community.

Admittedly, I generally have moments of confidence, happily more and more of them, with only occasional moments of hesitancy or misgiving. My doubt is nevertheless honest and, I insist, an important component of a genuine religious or, if you prefer, spiritual commitment. Doubt is neither disturbing nor dangerous.

I view doubt and skepticism as aids to serious discussion about convictions regarding Deity and meaning, and I am not alone in doing so. I am part of a tradition that refuses to kill the head in order to express what the heart may want or need. Our hearts may wish for simplicity and certainty and want our thoughts always to be in alignment, but such an outcome would lead to the end of all conflict and confusion about beliefs and behaviors.

I believe it is not an accident that the name linked to the spiritual quest for much of Western religious thought is Israel,[1] for its meaning in Hebrew includes the notion of conflict and struggle. This suggests we put greater priority on asking the right questions than in confidence that there is a definite, unwavering answer to life's most important challenges. That perspective, however disappointing to some, both describes our existential situation and gives us license for free and fearless inquiry.

There are some who insist we must silence doubt, for if the "doubt-virus" be allowed to multiply, we will never achieve or embrace certainty. There are others who would encourage us to abandon the effort since it will never lead to an absolute resolution. To my mind, the journey is the prize, for the opposite of faith is not doubt. The more dangerous posture, not merely to God or in religious communities, is indifference. The poem "Sing Out" may clarify:

> Praise me, says God;
> I will know that you love me.
> Curse me, says God;
> I will know that you love me.
> Sing out my graces, says God.
> Raise your fist against me and revile.
> Sing out my praises or revile.
> Reviling is also a kind of praise, says God.
> But if you sit fenced off
> in your apathy, says God.
> If you sit entrenched in:
> "I don't give a hang."
> If you look at the stars and yawn,

If you see suffering and don't cry out,
If you don't praise and don't revile,
Then I created you in vain, says God.[2]

There was a time, not so long ago, when representatives of many religious traditions trumpeted what they labeled as *proofs* for the existence of God. The current scholarly preference is to describe these "proofs," however persuasive or ineffectual, as arguments. Rather than offering incontrovertible proof for the independent reality of God, they, at best, point in a coherent and provocative direction. I offer two examples.

The first argument builds on the notion that human beings seem hardwired for morality. We have an intrinsic sense of right and wrong. Every society that we know of has embraced the conviction that murder is wrong even if different groups have defined murder differently. For instance, murder was illegal in Nazi Germany, but the elimination of certain categories of people was not murder because these specific groups did not fall under the legal protection of citizenship and were not considered persons at all. Murder was still morally and legally wrong, but only if the victim were considered to belong to the human family.[3]

The argument makes a leap: if there are universal standards, there must be an extrinsic source. Or, in religious terms, there must be a standard beyond self and society, one that humans divine, even if imperfectly.

An evolutionary biologist might object that our moral qualities are simply the outcome of biological adaptation. But that, at most, describes how morals occur. It is an insufficient answer as to why morality is a substantive part of the human package, why we are compelled to make moral decisions on a host of behaviors, with our responses ranging from sacrifice and altruism to selfishness and solipsism. Those decisions impact all our interactions, all the time.

This argument insists that we label specific behaviors as benevolent or malevolent out of something more than personal taste or some primal and mindless biological instinct. It suggests there is something built into us, something larger than self, something that, while it cannot be proved, suggests a connection, however reluctantly or even enthusiastically expressed, to a divine source.

The second argument is known as the argument from design, even by those who reject it out of hand. If for no other reason than its lengthy pedigree, it deserves some attention and reflection.

Some 1,800 years ago, the Jewish sage, Rabbi Akiba, affirms, "As a house implies a builder, a dress a weaver, a door a carpenter, so the world proclaims God, its Creator."[4] This notion conforms to general experience. Whenever we recognize a pattern or design, we confidently conclude there must be a designer. Spell that with a capital D, and voilà!

In our time, many scientists find no room or need for Deity in their considerations, theories, or laws, yet there is much in contemporary physics that provides fodder for spiritual reflection. Quantum physics seems confusing, even to many who call themselves quantum physicists, but I know of no more elegant description of the argument then this one:

> One intriguing observation that has bubbled up from physics is that the universe seems calibrated for life's existence. If the force of gravity were pushed upward a bit, stars would burn out faster, leaving little time for life to evolve on the planets circling them. If the relative masses of protons and neutrons were changed by a hair, stars might never be born, since the hydrogen they eat wouldn't exist. If, at the Big Bang, some basic numbers—the "initial conditions"—had been jiggled, matter and energy would never have coagulated into galaxies, stars, planets or any other platform stable enough for life as we know it.[5]

Of course, there is an element of circular reasoning in that depiction. The manner in which we experience the world suggests repetition and pattern. Therefore, we conclude that is proof of the accuracy of our experience and the independent presence of design and, perhaps, a Designer. A further challenge may be found in the recognition that there are moments when the universe seems more chaotic than ordered, when the notion of design may appear altogether absent.

Against that challenge, we have Charles Darwin, who says: "If we consider the whole universe, the mind refuses to look upon it as the outcome of chance—that is, without design or purpose."[6] And Einstein offers a similar rumination in a remarkable excerpt, found in a lengthy interview he gave shortly after his fiftieth birthday:

> We are in the position of a little child entering a huge library filled with books in many languages. The child knows someone must have written those books. It does not know how. It does understand the language in which they are written. The child dimly suspects a mysterious order in the arrangement of the books but does not know what it is. That, it seems to me, is the attitude of even the most intelligent human being toward God. We see the universe marvelously arranged and obeying certain laws but only dimly understand these laws.[7]

With Einstein's vivid imagery in mind, I trust you will concur that neither doubt nor certainty eliminate the prospect for discussion or argument, and that suggests that reflections about Deity are worthy of study and, perhaps, affirmation.

FOR FURTHER REFLECTION:

1. How may doubt be a positive instrument for you in the service of inquiry?
2. What are the strengths and weaknesses of the two arguments presented in this chapter— the presence of a moral impulse and the notion of design—as evidence for God?
3. What is your own best argument or evidence to persuade someone to affirm God or to conclude to the contrary?

CHAPTER 11

So Many Names for God

No words are adequate in naming Deity, yet we try.

W E MOVE NOW FROM science and what Einstein describes as the search for "laws" to material that is less susceptible to precise measurement. Just as it does regarding miracles, the Bible provides insights to enhance our awareness of, appreciation for, and engagement with reflections about Deity. That includes passages that focus on the many names for and the unique designation of what we often simply refer to as "God."

You may have heard that Inuit and Yupik cultures have an extraordinary number of words for snow. I have seen estimates as high as 500. And even though that interpretation is disputed or discredited, depending on which scholars one relies, it provides an intriguing direction for this discussion. Be it fact or fable, just consider the wisdom (or whimsy) of this reflection from *The Mother Tongue* by Bill Bryson.[1] After asserting that "Eskimos,"[2] by his count, have fifty words for snow, he continues:

> The Italians, as we might expect, have over 500 names for different types of macaroni . . . The residents of . . . Papua, New Guinea have

a hundred words for yams, while the Maori . . . have thirty-five for dung (don't ask me why).

The controlling phrase above is "as we might expect," for its logic depends on an awareness that Italian tradition has a long and profound relationship with pasta. Presumably, that same logic applies to Inuit and Yupik vocabulary, as well as the residents of New Guinea and New Zealand. Their environments provide the context for language and, more immediately, for distinctions that may not make sense to us. By that, I do not mean they are silly. Rather, we do not recognize or register the differences among fifty types of snow. We don't possess the cognitive software to process that data.

Even should it be valid only in the realm of poetry and metaphor, the parallel in biblical tradition is the extraordinary number of names that the text and subsequent tradition assign to Deity. Islam specifically articulates ninety-nine names for what in English is simply labeled God.

Why so many names? The best explanation is that the Hebrew experience, continued in Islam, was of a God-intoxicated or, to use less-provocative language, a meaning-obsessed environment. Primitive or precise, and however inadequate the language, the Hebrews experienced and described understandings of those experiences in words and, in doing so, conveyed an awareness of a sacred dimension around them and in them. In fact, they seemed compelled not only to speak but also to assign a name or names to what they encountered in those moments, if for no other reason than to help them remember. I would argue that the abundance of names reflects an acute recognition that no word or phrase alone is sufficient to capture the meaning and awe of a confrontation with something or someone defined as sacred. So we inherit a range of names, which reflect a spectrum of collisions with holiness. Against the limits of language to describe these encounters, biblical tradition offers a cornucopia. All of these appellations still cannot capture fully either the encounter with Deity or the meaning of that experience, but the Bible insists that it is invaluable to make the effort to do so.

The remarkable range and depth of those encounters with holiness are illustrated by a commentary that begins with a skeptic challenging a sage: "Why did God appear to Moses in a thorn bush?" The sage replies:

> Were it a carob or a sycamore, you would ask the same question, but to dismiss you without a reply is not right . . . To teach you that no place is devoid of God's presence, not even a thorn bush.[3]

In brief, the commentary asserts that no matter what the name applied to an experience believed to be of or in the presence of Deity, there is no place where God is not. That may serve as an entry point to shift from the plethora of names for experiences with Deity to Jewish tradition's other assertion. Namely, one appellation stands alone in bringing us closer to the meaning in and a meeting with the divine.[4] That declaration may capture the core spirit of a *New Testament* episode in which Jesus responds to a question about what constitutes the most important commandment. In the Gospel of Mark, Chapter 12:29-31, Jesus answers, "Hear, O Israel: the Lord our God , the Lord is One." Known in Jewish tradition as the *Shema*, the statement does not present itself as a commandment or order but rather as a call to awareness. Then Jesus continues by citing something that more correctly fits the description of a command. "Love your neighbor as yourself. There is no commandment greater than *these*" (Italics added).

We shall return to the matter of neighbors. For the moment, I want to reflect on the first part of Jesus' reply, especially because the *Shema* includes what rabbinic tradition insists is the most vital and intimate name for what we call God. It is variously translated as "Listen Israel—the people, the tribes, the nation, the fellowship, the patriarch, all of those—the Eternal is our God. The Eternal is One."[5]

No matter what the precise translation or interpretation, the place of the *Shema* in my tradition demands attention. And while I'll not explore all possibilities, it seems noteworthy that the phrase in the *Shema*, "The

Eternal is One," indicates that life, with its vagaries and challenges, may not always seem clear or make sense, but that is not equivalent to saying it doesn't have meaning at all times.

A deeper suggestion is that in Hebrew "one" has another nuance, one that implies more than a single unit. Specifically, *Echad* may also suggest alone, as in only. The Eternal is the only reality, all there is.

Imagine, for the moment, that the ocean is the only thing there is.[6] Consider all of reality, the entire universe, everything subsumed in the ocean. Of course, there are waves. By definition, waves are part of the ocean before they become waves, while they are waves, and after they disappear from view. The ocean is analogous to the ground of being, out of which all life emerges. The ocean is God. And for a moment there is a wave, perhaps called Michael. Michael was part of the ocean before he *was*, part of the ocean while he *is*, and he is still part of the ocean after he departs from view.

Alas, waves in the form of Michaels, Lydias, Kims, and Alexanders seem to have difficulty with two life challenges. These waves are not always successful at remembering and living as though they are always part of the ocean, part of God. Secondly, because we are part of God, we are connected to all the other waves, all the manifestations of the divine. Unfortunately, while we inhabit bodies we constantly experience ourselves as separate, distinct, and apart when clearly we are never without God and unconnected with each other.[7]

Some may criticize this analysis as warmed-over pantheism. For if God is all there is, then good and evil, wisdom and foolishness, are categories without significance or meaning. No distinctions are appropriate or possible; whatever is and whatever will be are nothing more than manifestations of Deity. There is no point in attempting to bridge the distance between the world as it is and the world as it should or ought to be.

What saves this effort from those challenges is the conviction that the language used in the description neither defines nor exhausts that which one may rightly say or encounter with regard to the source of all experience, even as conviction and logic lead me to conclude that behind all appearances, behind the awesome diversity of life, there is always only the One.

Including pantheism in this discussion is not equivalent to embracing it. That is the insight explicit in a song attributed to Rabbi Levi Yitzchak of Berdichev.[8] One of the giants of Hasidism, he was often and inaccurately attacked for his alleged pantheism. This song, called the *Dudele*, describes an affectionate, intimate, even stunning familiarity with the subject. He sings to an audience of One, although we are invited to listen in.

> Master of the Universe,
> Let me sing a song for You a song.
> Where can I find You?
> And where can I not find You?
> For wherever I go, You go too.
> Where I stay, You stay too.
> Always You, only You.
> Again You, only You.
> When things are good—You.
> And not so well—You . . .
> The heavens—You.
> Earth—You.
> Above—You.
> Below—You.
> Where I turn—You and where I stir—You.
> You! You! You! You.

What extricates Levi Yitzchak from the limiting suggestion of pantheism is his absolute conviction that no words can contain God, for God is more than all there is. To use the argot of theology, pantheism asserts that God is in everything. Levi Yitzchak's song turns that category on its head. Not God is in everything, rather everything is in God.[9] The Rabbi's experience of divine imminence is so overwhelming that it becomes the foundation for an awesome encounter with transcendence, with the wholly other, the Holy One, that which is beyond the capacity of all or any words to capture.

Through the centuries, a long and illustrious list of writers, aware of the inadequacy of words alone, nonetheless use words to point us toward an understanding of and confidence in the conviction that God is, God matters, and, indeed, God matters ultimately. And those innumerable attempts to convey the ineffable have led to a remarkable and intimate collection of names in an effort, ultimately insufficient, to describe and define the indescribable.

FOR FURTHER REFLECTION:

1. Are you able to recall moments that included an encounter with awe, such that words fail to capture the experience fully?
2. How did those moments impact or change you?
3. How do you hold such experiences in mind or heart?

CHAPTER 12

The Limits of Language about the Divine

While words are insufficient to describe any real or imagined encounters with Deity, words are all we have.

IF THE EFFORT TO express what we mean by invocations about Deity means anything substantive, it insists that our effort is to describe, however challenging both in language and in fact, what constitutes ultimate reality. Embracing that effort comes with an obstacle—namely all descriptions fall short and are inadequate. In effect, all language is metaphor, by which I mean words point to and suggest something about reality but cannot convey its full essence, whether the controversial matter at hand be real or delusion.

Too often, defenders of the God idea present their reflections as if they were providing objective information. But I am aware that this discussion tells you more about my experience than what I may assert as dispassionate, unbiased, or authentic description of divinity. At best, what we express says more about our personal experience than the objective nature of reality. Simply stated, language is not up to the task.

With that in mind, I may as well risk a bit more controversy. In Judaism, the quintessential encounter with God occurs at Mount Sinai. No one knows precisely where Sinai is, and the scriptural chronology and the content of God's revelation to Moses on the mountain are confusing. But something happened. That much is sure, whether you believe it was a full-blown and mass epiphany, or a collective hallucination, or a scam perpetrated by a cabal of ancient charlatans. The memory of standing at that mountain forever changed a particular people, and the record of their experience continues to impact the world. What happened was far more an experience of presence than of content.

The Hebrew Bible speaks of that event. But the text, I argue, is at a remove from the experience itself. It describes the effect of the revelation, the human response to the encounter, but it does not and cannot capture the event itself. Perhaps that is the meaning of a rabbinic commentary that says the people heard only the first letter of the first word in the *Decalogue*.[1] The first letter is an *Aleph*, which in Hebrew has no sound. So, in effect, they heard silence. This must mean the Israelites encountered and recognized an experience far more than they heard specific instructions.

At minimum, language gets in the way with both the challenge of translation and, more importantly, the limits of discourse. However, many apologists for religion insist that the language, in this or whatever other text they wish literally to preserve and to preserve it literally, precisely circumscribes this or any other revelation.

With such limits of language, the most we may assert confidently regarding the Israelite experience at Sinai is that God *is*. Or as the great twentieth-century theologian Franz Rosenzweig[2] describes the revelation at Mount Sinai is that God came down. That suggests the people encountered a moment of (what to call it?) clarity. More precisely, he writes, "All that God ever revealed in revelation is revelation."[3] When the Israelites leave that place,[4] they can't help themselves. They are compelled to speak about the encounter, not only of what they experienced but also of what it means. Yet that is once removed from the encounter itself. The text, as we have it, is a consequence of the event, an elaboration after the fact, not an objective eyewitness record of the meeting itself. I recognize that this is not a commonplace understanding. In fact, it suggests that much of traditional practice is a result of human reflection about God and not necessarily a representation of direct imperatives. For many, that marks these comments (and me) as heretical.

Why not, then, offer an illustration likely to get me into even more trouble?

No doubt, some readers recall the name Charles Colson. He served as special counsel to President Nixon, from 1969 to 1973, and is more famously known as one of the few White House insiders who served prison time for his part in the Watergate scandal.

Shortly before Colson was scheduled to begin incarceration, his life seemingly ruined, and despite having taken pride in the sobriquet "Nixon's Hatchet Man," he had a life-altering experience. Whatever actually happened, there is no question a transformation in character was the outcome.

I remember hearing Colson speak at length and passionately at a Rotary Club luncheon, as he described a late-night encounter in his car with Jesus. Several of my table companions expressed some discomfort that I might take offense at his unapologetic evangelizing. On the contrary, I was intrigued.

A strong argument certainly may be made that Colson's encounter was desperate and delusional, the experience of a man at a psychological breaking point. A reflection by the poet Christian Wiman, from *My Bright Abyss*, seems apropos: "That conversions often happen after or during intense life experiences, especially traumatic experiences, is sometimes used as evidence against them." [5] Or, as I was reminded by a listener of the radio show I co-host with representatives of Protestantism and Roman Catholicism,[6] I once said, "There is no end to the outrageous things our minds can invent and then go on to believe."

Nonetheless, I ascribe credence to Colson's experience. Invoking Jesus is the language he knows and the language in which his mind registers, recognizes, and, most significantly, remembers what he experienced.

My difficulty with Colson's description, as it would be with any other similar expression, is his absolute conviction, the certainty that his way is the only way to have a transcendent life-changing encounter. In effect, he argues that not only is his language the best description but also that the description defines the uniquely correct and only possible way to encounter the divine. No other position has similar validity. Alternative expressions, at best, are mere shadows of his exclusive and precise view. But that position elevates one's religion into a God-like idolatry, rather than understanding it to be a language pointing to the Ultimate, for which no words are sufficient and no single symbol system may presume, univocally, to contain or convey. To suggest otherwise is not dissimilar to the obviously false conviction that English is better than French. More immediately, one would assert (wrongly) that not only is English superior, but it is also the only authentic way to speak, think, write, and understand. St. Augustine's challenging reflection comes to mind: "If you think you have understood God, it is not God."[7]

With that in mind, it is no small matter that the Hebrew Bible presents convincing evidence against a univocal position. Had I written the text, I likely would have argued for a particularistic or triumphalist view, one that insists our language and, more critically, our way of life to be the one true path. But the text knows better as it presents more than a few examples of non-Jews,[8] who have an authentic connection with the Holy One despite the fact that they are not members of our particular club or tribe. For the moment, the point isn't whether such a connection exists for them or anyone as it is the unwillingness of Tanakh[9] to declare that any group may have a monopoly on Deity. Or, to cite Christian Wiman once more, "[t]he trouble comes when the effort to name and know an experience replaces the experience itself."[10]

Any serious commentary about religion must keep that warning in mind. Yet one must also acknowledge that words are the essential tool in the effort to explain one's experience and to share it. While of a different order of magnitude, the Prophet Jeremiah's compulsion, what he describes as "a fire in my bones,"[11] is not a foreign experience for so many who express both the necessity and frustration to describe an encounter with the power that resides at the heart of all life. So, yes, language, even with its frustrations and limitations, matters.

FOR FURTHER REFLECTION:

1. When words fail to express your feelings or experiences, what do you do and how do you respond?
2. If you have had encounters with persons from a different faith or tradition than your own, in what ways did that experience enrich your faith journey or growth in spirit?
3. Similarly, if you've experienced someone trying to convert you to their religion, how did it make you feel and how did you respond?
4. Would you respond the same way again?

CHAPTER 13

Any Word Spoken in
True Sincerity

Deity has an intimate proper name, but it isn't easily articulated or understood.

I N BIBLICAL TRADITION, names matter. That is why the text regularly provides elaborations, most often word plays on why someone receives a specific name. For example, Adam connects with the Hebrew word for earth, *Adama*. As for Eve, the text links the meaning of her name to the Hebrew word for life. The Hebrew pronunciation, *Chava*, is a variation on *Chaim*—life. Abraham is understood to mean "father of multitudes," which is both an irony, in light of the birth challenges in his story, and a biblical conceit that from him descend many distinct kinship groups or tribes. Cain is named by his mother, Eve, as she declares, "I have acquired (or made) a person with God's help."[1] Provocatively, with regard to Cain's brother, Abel, the text provides no attempt at explanation or derivation for his name. Perhaps this is a clue to how we might frame the story that follows, in which Abel is killed by Cain and becomes the first murder victim in the Bible. The name Abel translates as a "puff of wind," hardly a name to suggest any significant parental ambitions for a child. In fact, that designation is one of the many occasions when the full biblical narrative provides a signpost or warning to be careful, especially about a literal reading of any story.

Many families continue this focus on choosing a name as they struggle to determine just the right option for a newborn. Do we honor so and so, remember that beloved deceased family member, or find an unusual designation? For an older generation, Johnny Cash's "A Boy Named Sue" comes to mind. Frank Zappa named a child Moom Unit and Gwyneth Paltrow chose Apple for her daughter. Some imagine that the appropriate choice will determine the child's direction, capacity, achievement, and personality, while others might argue this concentration, even obsession, is little more than magical thinking.

The matter of names, when applied to God in the Jewish tradition, points us to Moses. While we previously explored details of his experience at the burning bush,[2] a vital biblical source for the importance of the God's name may be found in the *content* of that encounter. Moses, not exactly excited with the job prospects that Deity places before him— "Come, therefore, I will send you to Pharaoh, and you shall free My people"—seems desperate to throw out objections, including this seeming non-sequitur: "When I come to the Israelites and say to them, The God of your ancestors has sent me . . . and they ask, What is His name? What shall I say to them?"[3] Whatever the limits of language, that query has to mean that such information must really matter.

As the Exodus text insists, Deity reveals *Deity's* most intimate proper name. For the Bible, as you likely know, God is not a sufficient designation for (what word to use?) God. It would be equivalent to calling a person "human being" rather than by his or her specific name. With all of our sophistication and learning, we often conclude that we have little to learn from a supposedly more primitive time. Yet it seems nothing less than extraordinary that God's personal name might offer a world of insight, not only into the biblical mindset but also for contemporary reflection.

We are speaking, then, of the "tetragrammaton," a scholarly term that refers to the four-letter name for God: YH . . . VH. You may also have encountered a variety of expressions, like Jehovah, Lord, or just The Name, all of which are diversions from or substitutes for whatever the precise articulation of the Hebrew might have been. In fact, Jewish tradition takes the word so seriously that one never pronounces it, and we remain unsure about the correct way to say it at all, hence, the description that may translate as "the name that is not spoken."

Adding the hypothetically correct vowels, A and E, to the four Hebrew letters, YH . . . VH, gets us to *Yah . . . Veh*. As to its meaning, you may be familiar with variations of "I am who I am" and "I will be what I will be." Apologies for any flashbacks to English grammar nightmares, but the name, as we have it, conforms to the third-person future tense of the verb *to be*, which in English means he/she/it will be. That suggests a seemingly heretical concept of God not yet being, as in not complete. But there is an even deeper prospect, for biblical Hebrew doesn't really have a future tense. In fact, it is a comparatively simple language (although I know many who have tried to master it would disagree with that assessment). The primary difficulty resides in the Hebrew alphabet. Once mastered, the language, which is based on a limited cadre of verbs, yields to memorization and to an awareness that Hebrew vocabulary develops through variations on its mainly three-letter verb roots.

With that in mind, the Bible's lack of or indifference to a future tense means it only knows two states—namely completed action and incompleted action. To be clear, completed action would be a statement like "he ran." That describes an event in the past. If not in that formulation or expression, I would need to report that "he is running." And here English demonstrates a remarkable sophistication, as well as an economy of language. For the statement, "He is running," means that as I make the observation, I am describing an event that happened, is happening, and will go on after I finish with the statement. Otherwise, I would say simply and accurately, "He ran." In effect, incompleted action allows me to say in just three words: he was, is, and will be running.[4]

Applying this to God's name yields the notion that God was, is, and will be. More precisely parallel to English, we might say, "God is *Ising*" or, if it seems clearer and you prefer, *Isnessing*. In effect, the name appears rich with the conviction that God is the energy of and in all existence. Was, is, and will be mean all life shares the same force. Or as a theologian friend writes, "Whatever makes each individual unique, that innermost core self, is precisely what we share with one another and our Creator. We are made of the same holy stuff."[5]

Coincidentally, as I write these words my radio is tuned to the local National Public Radio affiliate, which just played a promotional segment for an old feature called *This I Believe*. The spot included a rich radio voice intoning, "I believe God lives in the space between people." So do I. But I also believe that God, as evidenced in the meaning or meanings of Deity's special or personal name, may be found in the experience that bridges the distance not only between persons but also in ourselves. Simply put, the wholly infinite and the most intimate are one.

Perhaps that is why I experience wonder and reverence in what others may consider little more than coincidence. To wit, were one to try spelling the sounds of breathing, the closest one might get to an accurate reflection is *Yah*, the sound, or better letters for taking breath in, and *Veh*, the sound of letting breath out. Consider, as well, the basic meaning of inspiration and expiration. The former means to take in the breath; the latter, in addition to being a synonym for dying, has a core meaning of to give back or return the breath. That is the wisdom of an Hasidic master, when he reminds us we are God's *shofarot*.[6] We only move because the breath of life, of holiness, of Deity passes through us. In effect, that means our primary sound, the one all life shares, binds us to each other and to the One.

But an exploration of God's primary name involves danger, as it may lead some to conclude that there is magic and potency restricted to that unique, if mysterious pronouncement. The difficulty is by no means limited to those with what we might judge to be a superstitious bent. Rather, a trap lies in the seductive appeal that can raise a discussion about the meaning and content of God's name into a conviction that one group, more likely one's own particular group, has a monopoly on truth. That course inevitably leads to a type of idolatry as one elevates specific convictions, customs, and beliefs into certainties or absolutes—to the equivalent of Deity. Inevitably, that leads to the conclusion that there is only one way to believe and worship, only one way to behave. More accurately, the elements of convictions, customs, and beliefs constitute a path to attain holiness, not the destination itself.

That is why I find an instruction from a classic of the Yiddish stage, *The Dybbuk*,[7] compelling. While it does not fall into any normative category of religious literature, the play includes sacred elements and may enlarge an understanding of God's intimate, even "secret," name, one that leads to an exquisite reframing of commonplace and ordinary matters— namely the profane and secular realms are filled with miracle, also and always.

In the play, Rabbi Azriel attempts an exorcism of a dybbuk, or spirit, which has overtaken a young woman. Before the rite begins, he offers a lengthy soliloquy that includes four parts, each containing four components in scrics.[8]

In the first part, all places are holy, but especially holy is the land of Israel (after all, it is a Jewish story); all places in Israel are holy, but especially holy is Jerusalem; all places in Jerusalem are holy, but the most holy place is the Holy of Holies, the inner sanctum of the ancient Temple.

There follows the second series. All persons are holy; especially holy are the children of Israel; especially holy in Israel are the priests; the most holy is, of course, the High Priest.

In the third series, the rabbi declares, all times are holy; especially sacred are the holy days. The most holy day is the Sabbath. The most holy Sabbath is the one called Yom Kippur.

The sequence concludes with the declaration that all languages are holy with special holiness ascribed to Hebrew; all Hebrew words are holy, but most holy are the names of God; all names for God are holy, but the most holy is God's proper name, the four-letter name.

Once a year, on Yom Kippur afternoon, the most holy person entered the most holy place and uttered just one word, the most sacred and intimate name of God.

In any folk tradition, that describes a powerful time even one where the fate of the world hangs in the balance. I love to imagine that, had the rabbi's reflection stopped there, I might accept the historic description as accurate but reject the conclusion as little more than an offensive expression of chauvinism and, especially dangerous, a conviction about a particular group's monopoly on God.

Fortunately, the rabbi continues to articulate a vision that seems very much of this and every moment. The secret, he argues, is, any time may be Yom Kippur afternoon. Any place may serve as the Holy of Holies. Any person can be a high priest. And here is the extraordinary part: any word spoken in true sincerity; that is God's proper name.

Our lifelong task is to make that statement true. For in addition to a remarkable notion about where God may be found, the commentary matches a conviction, perhaps better, an obsession about the critical path to embrace fully the overwhelming miracle of life, our very brief moment of consciousness within eternity. Most profoundly expressed, the rabbi's discourse reminds us not only about the preciousness in every moment but also about how powerful and how linked to holiness, to God, every human action, every moment may be. The effort to live with that intensity, with that ecstasy, means embracing a path that fills life with meaning, wonder, and joy no matter what the circumstances. That means every moment has the capacity for us to recognize that we live with and in the presence of the divine. Further, like the rabbi in *The Dybbuk*, our words, especially when born of compassionate intensity, may point to, reflect, and even become aspects of God's intimate and profound signature or name.

With that in mind, consider Psalm 150.
Praise God with blasts of the horn;
praise God with harp and lyre.
Praise God with timbrel and dance;
praise God with lute and pipe.
Praise God with resounding cymbals;
praise God with loud-clashing symbols.
Let all that breathes praise God.
Hallelujah!

You may be aware that biblical poetry's primary modality is to divide a line into two parts, with comparable content in the A and B sections. For example, if a first stanza were to speak about dogs, the second part will offer some reference to a canine, be it some specific breed, a mutt, or a puppy. As applied to Psalm 150, the penultimate line either destroys the parallelism or is its culmination. All that has breath, the Psalm indicates, is a musical instrument, too, one which plays, breathes God. Hallelu . . . *Yah*, which, not surprisingly, is one of the many Hebrew names for Deity.

The Psalm's last lines recall Rabbi Abraham Isaac Kook's interpretation of the name Israel. Rather than associate the Jewish people's patronymic and intimate name with conflict,[9] Kook interprets the Hebrew to mean "he will sing God."[10] And that, I suspect, provides an intriguing window into a rich spiritual life. For while it is true that one can breathe without singing, one cannot sing without breathing. Yet there may be moments filled with stillness and intensity, moments that professional athletes and performers sometimes describe as being in flow. That may translate as when the boundaries between breathing and singing dissolve, and such an experience, that kind of "singing," is essential to our being, as it is the best description of being fully engaged, fully alive. That experience, one I hope is not unfamiliar to many readers, requires no words. Despite our best efforts, it is more than any name or extended description may ever hope fully to capture or convey. All of that and more are implicit in unpacking just some of the meaning(s) in what our biblical tradition insists is the direct and fulsome name for God. In those moments, we express the experience of standing on and being a part of holy ground.

FOR FURTHER REFLECTION:

1. What would you describe as the sacred elements in your most important relationships?
2. Are you able to identify any common threads in moments when you recognized that something sacred or transcendent was part of the experience?
3. Are there any experiences in your life that you might describe as an encounter with a "burning bush?"

CHAPTER 14

Would You Like to Buy Some Life Insurance?

The business of religion need not be variations of reassurance about what may await us at death, but rather a quest for wholeness and holiness in this life.

I HOPE THAT I HAVE made a case that all life shares the same source, existing because of and within that power. And even if we do not link that energy with ideas about Deity, we at least intuitively recognize the presence and absence of that life force. We use the word "death" to describe what we mean when the energy that resides within us leaves. With that departure, the container begins to disintegrate, literally to lose its integrity. For once the coordinating principle that animated us moves on, our bodies, like an abandoned home, begin to break down or, more precisely, return to their constituent elements.

A deeper and more honest response to the question of death is we really don't know what happens, at least not to us. That may be an unusual, if not an awkward, statement for someone in the religion "business." But even as this challenge has engaged humanity from the dawn of self-consciousness, the truth is I could suggest almost any proposition about what happens when we die. Both you and I know that I really don't know. So while I genuinely believe that we are always safe with God, or maybe more accurately, safe in God, I also recognize that even that proposition falls into the realm of speculation, if not wish fulfillment. Worst-case scenario, death is what it was like before we were born. So, unless one subscribes to notions about past lives and reincarnation, that means no more or less than the absence of an I, an end to ego as, like a dewdrop, we "slip into the sea."[1]

Nonetheless, most of us consider that the whole function of Western religious tradition is to assure followers they will get into God's world when they die, in other words, to guarantee eternal life for those who have membership in the only right club. For most folks, most of the time, the whole point of religion is, as it were, death insurance. That fearsome effort against annihilation is the reason some embrace a particular creed, as though it were the only thing that really mattered, while others, reflecting on the same content, view religion as no more than a crutch, a combination of superstition and vanity against the pathos of personal destruction.

I shall not deny that many traditions, my own not excepted, include denominations and creeds that contemplate afterlife as far more than just a hope or promise. But religion, taken seriously, isn't really about living forever. It is far more intent on how to get God into this world than it is on any certainty about providing an admission ticket into a next one. Bringing a sacred dimension into the here and now, that is humanity's purpose, literally our raison d'être.

That recalls an episode in the life of our troubled patriarch, Jacob. After fleeing the wrath of his brother, Esau, he arrives at a particular place,[2] one he will name Bethel, meaning house of God. According to the story, Jacob spends the night there and has a remarkable dream in which he sees a ladder reaching into the heavens, with angels going up and down.[3] Yet, to the extent we may consider such matters at all, the angels are traveling in the wrong order or direction. Angels are supposed to go down and then up. Unless, this dream is meant to remind and instruct that our deeds carry vital messages, so much so that we are also messengers or angels.[4] That is what we, like Jacob, are called to be. Even more remarkable, at least in the dream, Jacob sees God (and here is where matters get awesome) standing either on top of the ladder, beside him, or on him. The Hebrew allows for all of those options. Given my prejudice on such matters, the notion of God depending on us, metaphorically represented as standing on Jacob, vividly suggests that Deity needs us, a notion I find both moving and meaningful. That radical idea means no matter what we do for a living, our true profession, to recall the wisdom of the four-year-old child mentioned in Chapter 7, is to be a place where God shows through. That is our purpose, our calling, for as long as the energy at the heart of all life resides within us.

Any next life, if such there be, will take care of itself. I may occasionally shock some traditional believers with this perspective: suppose that God only allows admission to the "eternal life country club" to followers with the one correct membership card. Odds are my card is likely to be the only right one, as Judaism has been doing this "religion-thing" longer than any other Western tradition. But, I argue, if it means something to say notions of Deity and of love belong together, then a God with love for humankind, who would condemn to eternal damnation any of God's children just because they are in the wrong club, would cause me to turn in my membership card. For I would much prefer the company of those in hell than to spend eternity with such a monster.

If the true concern of religion is what we are doing here and now, how might we use our brief moment before eternity to make a difference here and now? What would justify our taking time, space, whatever portion may be ours, that at journey's end some might whisper, "Well done, well done"?

No matter what the desire or desperation for an afterlife we must acknowledge mystery, even as we understand this sardonic comment I've seen attributed to George Bernard Shaw: "Millions of people are worried about living forever, yet they wouldn't know what to do if they had a free weekend." Indeed, it seems the height of hubris to imagine there is something so important about your or my consciousness that we should go on, as it were, littering the universe forever (I admit a willingness to be surprised).

Physics provides an intriguing idea to inform the discussion. The first law of thermodynamics states that "energy can be changed from one form to another, but it cannot be created or destroyed."[5] That means the energy that made and makes me continues, even as the conclusion evokes Einstein's famous equation, $E = MC^2$.

I am far from alone in recognizing this equation to be a rich statement about the nature of ultimate reality, not only for physics but also for theology.[6] For it asserts that the energy of which we are, for a brief time, custodians does have a continuity, one might even say a life after us. $E = MC^2$ means that $M = E/C^2$. Mass divided by the square of the speed of light indicates that matter is simply energy sufficiently slowed down that we experience its mass, as solid, liquid, or gas. But we know that matter consists of far more (empty) space than any substance. Theoretically, I should be able to walk through a wall, even as the wall and everything else go through me. The important recognition is that the only thing that really exists is the energy or power that infuses us, that makes all life live. And that, I have previously argued, is Deity, the *Godness* in and all around us. Such is the teaching of a story that speaks of a brilliant young student challenged by his father, "I shall give you a kopek[7] if you can tell me where God is." The child's response, "I shall give you two kopeks if you can tell me where God is not."

Were I to place a wager, I'd go with the child. And for whatever time may be our allotted portion in this life, be it brief or lengthy, the journey is filled with meaning when we live out the conviction that we are always in the presence of the sacred. That includes while we *are* and after we no longer experience this experience, meaning we are dead. While we live, we need only to look and genuinely see that which is always around and in us. After all, there will be more than enough time to be dead, a very long time indeed. But as long as we are here, our life task is to bring a sacred dimension into our lives and, then, to share that presence and its consequence with others. That is the true essence of life insurance, namely insurance for a meaning-filled life.

FOR FURTHER REFLECTION:

1. What happens to your religious convictions in the absence of eternal life?
2. In analyzing the story of Jacob's dream, I suggested that God depends on us. If so, what are your most significant talents and skills for that interpretation?

CHAPTER 15

The Many and Miraculous Faces of God

Humanity's connection with the divine means we perceive God when we see each other.

A S I WRITE THESE comments, many in Western society are troubled deeply by what media describe as the rise of Islam or, in the more combative language of political discourse, "radical Islamic terrorism." Far too many assign the worst motives to all Muslims, as though there were no moderation in Islam and no accommodation possible with it. Such is the equivalent of the assertion, equally incorrect, that the historic, bigoted, and violent actions of the Ku Klux Klan offer proof of corruption in all expressions of Christianity.

Haxhi Dede Reshat Bardis, former head of the Bektashi movement, an offshoot of the Shia tradition in Islam, offers a different and compelling voice. His comments appear in *Besa: Muslims Who Saved Jews in World War II*,[1] a volume that chronicles the courageous work of Albanians during the Holocaust:

At the time of the Nazi occupation the Prime Minister of Albania was Medi Fasheri. He was a member of the Bektashi. He refused to release the names of Jews to the Nazi occupiers. He organized an underground of all Bektashi to shelter all the Jews, both citizens and refugees. At that time nearly one half of all Muslims in Albania were Bektashi. Prime Minister Fasheri gave a secret order: "All Jewish children will sleep with your children, all will eat the same food, all will live as one family."

We Bektashi see God everywhere, in every one. God is in every pore and every cell, therefore all are God's children. There cannot be infidels. There cannot be discrimination. If one sees a good face, one is seeing the face of God.

That last line echoes the Hebrew word "*Peniel.*" It means "face of God," which is the name Jacob gives to the location where he engaged in what may be the most important wrestling match ever, after which, he declares, "I have seen God face-to-face, yet my life was preserved."[2] Jacob also receives a new name, Israel, which in biblical parlance always signals a transformative encounter. Accordingly, in just about every translation of the Genesis story we are instructed that Jacob wrestled with an "Angel."[3] You may be familiar with the traditional instruction that no one can see God's face and survive the encounter. That is likely why most English translations of this full episode substitute *divine being* in place of the word "God" in order to finesse the need for further explanation concerning Jacob's survival.

However, the original Hebrew is unambiguous. The word in the text is "*Elohim,*"[4] which means God. So the obvious challenge, did Jacob encounter a person or did he see God? The unequivocal biblical response is yes.

Jacob, like all of us, emerges from life's turmoil and challenges wounded or, according to the text, limping. Nonetheless, the sun rises to greet him as he welcomes a new day as he passes on to the next face-of-God moment and the next.

In fact, just a few verses later, Jacob meets his brother Esau. After an absence of some twenty years, they embrace and weep. In that encounter, the text has Jacob articulate a bold equation. In translation, the controlling verse indicates "to see your face is [equal to] seeing the face of God."[5]

That means, when we really see and really embrace the other, especially when moving from alienation to connection, we experience the highest and the holiest encounter possible.

That conviction may also explain why the text continues to address the patriarch as both Jacob and Israel. Had I composed the story, my happily-ever-after impulse would have indicated a complete transformation in Jacob's circumstance and character. Finally, now all will be well. But both the text and experience recognize that isn't how life unfolds. Once Jacob becomes Israel, he does not or (more accurately) cannot live always with new awareness or commitment. He does not always rise, but even when he is "just" Jacob, he is forever changed.

Forever linked to Jacob and eponymously to a specific people, the name "Israel" is, of course, laden with significance. Not surprisingly, the first interpretation occurs at the very moment of bestowing the new name. You are Israel "because you have striven with beings divine and human and have prevailed."[6] The link is in the consonance of the Hebrew pronunciation, *Yisrael*, with the verb *Saritha*, which may be translated as you wrestled, struggled, or as in this example, "you have striven." More problematic is the notion of prevailed because the root of the Hebrew word is "YKL," which generally suggests competence and capacity, as in the Israeli street phrase, "*Yakol Lehiyot*," meaning it's possible, could be.

In short, an appropriate interpretation of Yisrael offers something less than notions of conquest. It suggests, especially helpful for our purposes, that Israel means you struggle with God and other people (what serious person doesn't have challenges with both subjects?) and you are able or competent to do so.

Earlier, I referred to an alternative meaning of the name "Israel," one attributed to Rabbi Abraham Isaac Kook.[7] Since Kook had a deep commitment to nonviolence, he disagreed that conflict would be expressed as the origin point for the name of his people. So he parsed the Hebrew in an alternative form, one that authentically translates Israel as "he will sing God."[8] The wonderful inference is that our song, with all its variations, is most authentic when we recognize that the lyric at its heart consists of just one remarkable word—God. Our lives should give evidence that the sum of our best efforts breathes the connection between all and the source of all. Or, to recall William Blake's reflection, "if the doors of perception were cleansed, everything would appear . . . as it is, infinite."[9] At such moments, an individual and/or people, no matter the religion or lack thereof, may become what it means to be Israel. When an individual sings that singular lyric, he or she sings God. He or she meets the face of God. Perhaps a time may come when all will share that lyric.

Kook's commentary breathes a universe of meaning. But my reflections fall short of accurately conveying his content. Perhaps, the following may get a bit closer, and while it uses the vocabulary of Christian tradition, I cannot but see the connection and be moved.

It is hard to imagine an effort to wrestle with issues of spirituality without referring to St. Francis of Assisi. And while no record exists of Francis having made this statement, it fits his spirit so precisely that he should have done so: "Preach the Gospel at all times and, when necessary, use words." That instruction, ostensibly offered to his followers, may inform us all. In brief, our lives must connect to and inspire others, for in that connection lies the power of transformation. All that is necessary is for us to do the work, which, not surprisingly, in Hebrew also means worship.

It may be objected that encountering God is the business of prophets and saints, not us common folk. No doubt, the categories of prophet and saint deserve our respect, maybe even awe. But there is an aspect of holiness accessible to all.

Chapter 6 of Judges offers what may be a less-visited biblical episode, but it also likely enhances the connection between humanity, Deity, and the miraculous capacity within us. A young man named Gideon surreptitiously prepares the wheat harvest in order to hide it from marauding raiders, identified in the text as Midianites. Suddenly an Angel greets him, "The Eternal is with you, valiant warrior!"[10] Instead of fear or disbelief about either the sudden interruption or the comment—our "valiant warrior," in fact, has no experience with battle—Gideon fires back with an ancient version of "who are you kidding":

> Please, my lord, if the Eternal is with us, why has this befallen us? Where are all [the] wondrous deeds about which our ancestors told us, saying, "Truly the Eternal brought us up out of Egypt"? Now the Eternal has abandoned us and delivered us into the hands of Midian!"

Gideon requests some divine intervention. Specifically, a few verses later, he asks for confirmation in the form of a wonder or sign.[11] His point: we could use a little help here. However, the response, which seems to ignore Gideon's request for a miraculous intervention, is an equally important variation of "seems like a great idea. That's why I've decided to send you." Gideon's assignment is the essential point. The Hebrew word, "*malach*," regularly translated as angel, comes to English as a variant for the Greek *angelos*. Neither in Hebrew nor in Greek does the word require any link to winged celestial beings. As I mentioned earlier, it simply means messenger.

So are we perhaps messengers who have forgotten our message?[12] And might that message include that there is a spark of divine fire in all, one that means our task is much more substantial than an awareness of the divine or, echoing Part 1 of this book, believing in miracles. It is to recognize and act upon our capacity to make clear the miracle of God's presence in all and to share that conviction with more and more of us.

That is the remarkable, if hidden, message in this legend from the Holocaust, which appears in a collection entitled *Hasidic Tales of the Holocaust*.[13] It began to circulate among rabbi Abraham Mordecai Alter's followers after his spectacular escape from the Warsaw ghetto:

The British Prime Minister, Winston Churchill, invited the . . . Rabbi . . . to come see him and advise him how to bring about Germany's downfall. The Rabbi gave the following reply: "There are two possible ways, one involving natural means, the other supernatural. The natural means would be if a million angels with flaming swords were to descend on Germany and destroy it. The supernatural would be if a million Englishmen parachuted down on Germany and destroyed it." Since Churchill was a rationalist, he chose the strategy based on natural means, angels with flaming swords.

The story's reversal of what constitutes natural and supernatural is the point. Each of us, like angels, with or without wings or swords, can be a place where others come to see the face of God, which seems to me quite simply miraculous. Yet there is more to the story and more in us.

In addition to being miracles, we have another skill: to make miracles happen. The tale points out, however subtly, that we are called to be representatives of holiness, more precisely for God. We have a superior, even supernatural endowment, namely to be a place where something of God shows through. In effect, making that gift manifest is a lifelong mission, one that only waits for us to "report for duty."[14] And when we do, we not only embrace an ideal but act upon that insight, so much so that we may ignite a flame that warms and inspires ourselves and others.

Similarly, consider Moses' so-called farewell speech in Deuteronomy. The content is peppered with a phrase that either makes no sense or, more compelling, unlocks a world of meaning. Repeated at least four times,[15] the specific comment is, "You saw with your own eyes." What surrounds that statement are references to the wonders and marvels of the Exodus drama, as in this critical example:

Moses summoned all Israel and said to them: You have seen all that the Eternal did before your very eyes in the land of Egypt, to Pharaoh and to all his courtiers and to his whole country: the wondrous feats that you saw with your own eyes, those prodigious signs and marvels. Yet to this day the Eternal has not given you a mind to understand or eyes to see or ears to hear. I led you through the wilderness forty years; the clothes on your back did not wear out, nor did the sandals on your feet.[16]

An obvious problem arises. The setting of Deuteronomy means Moses addresses people who could not have seen what he is describing, as the imagined or real time frame for the text is forty years after the Exodus. Speaking for the final time, Moses confronts a new generation that did not experience the great drama of liberation from slavery. Indeed, the text, especially the last verse, seemingly goes out of its way to make either absurd or wondrous insight available. Taken as a matter of fact, the notion of such remarkably long-lasting clothing and shoes sets a whole new and impossible standard for durability. That provides the comic element made explicit in a compilation of rabbinic sources on these verses:

> Rabbi Shimon bar Yochai's son, Rabbi Elazar, asked his father-in-law, "How did the Israelites clothe themselves in the wilderness; did they take their looms and other instruments out of Egypt to weave garments for themselves?"
>
> His father-in-law, Rabbi Shimon ben Yossi, replied, "At the giving of the Torah, the angels gave the Israelites garments which never wore out."
>
> "But what if they needed new clothes because they gained or lost weight; and didn't the children need larger garments as they grew?" Rabbi Elazar wanted to know.
>
> "They never needed new garments," replied Rabbi Shimon, "for their clothes grew with them. Don't be amazed, for you find a similar occurrence in nature. Doesn't a snail's shell grow along with it?"
>
> "However," inquired Rabbi Elazar, "didn't the Israelites have to wash these clothes sometimes?"

"The Clouds of Glory used to rub them until they were clean and white," explained Rabbi Shimon.

"But the Clouds of Glory were of fire," objected Rabbi Elazar. "Didn't they burn the garments?"

"They were heavenly garments," replied Rabbi Shimon, "and therefore were not scorched by the Clouds."

"And weren't the Israelites infested with lice because they were leading a squalid desert life?" He questioned.

"Certainly not!" replied his father-in-law. "If the corpses of the generation which heard God's voice at Mount Sinai were not touched by worms, certainly insects did not bother them while they were alive."

"And didn't garments absorb the odor of perspiration, since they were never changed?" Rabbi Elazar continued to ask.

"They were saved from that also," responded Rabbi Shimon. "The Well of Miriam caused sweet smelling grass to sprout. When the Israelites rested . . . they became scented with the sweet perfume."[17]

The twists and turns of this stunning conversation seem to be a tongue-in-cheek way of pointing out that if one needs to go to such lengths to defend a literal rendering of a text, something else, something deeper, may be in play. Far more than any subtle clue, the commentary provides critical evidence that the controlling verse of this section of Torah is, "Yet to this day the Eternal has not given you a mind to understand or eyes to see or ears to hear." Moses' statement seems to apply to them. The lesson also applies to us, as we are so often blind to the essential teaching that not only are miracles always present, but also the overwhelming miracle of a divine presence resides in us and is always available to us. We just need to understand in order to see and hear "what is there about us always."[18] The urgency of this chapter is for us to live out the conviction that we are the heart of the story. We are the many faces of Deity, the foremost miracle of God. When we recognize that gift, then any place and every moment merits the designation *Peniel*—namely, we find ourselves in and with the face of God.

Even if it may sound a little preachy, that message, a key to celebrating the miracle of life, may reside in our willingness to respond to another biblical imperative—namely "You shall be holy for I the Eternal your God am holy."[19] Aside from the bold assertion that humanity shares, at least potentially, some sacred God stuff, the Hebrew may be translated in an outrageous or, as I prefer to conclude, precious way. "You shall be holy, [*so that*] I the Eternal your God am holy." Imagine the awesome power, then, in what we do or fail to do. How we care or fail to care. When we inspire or ridicule, not only does that touch someone else, but it also impacts the power at the heart of the universe, the heart of all life, that which we call God. Some of my argument may seem to echo aspects of the assertion of Chapter 7, namely that human beings are of infinite and sacred value. However, that is far from the bottom line. Rather, the burden of the discussion now is a conviction that we are not only invaluable, but we are also, and more singularly, the essential vehicle in which the divine may be confirmed and encountered.

I take that contention seriously. And taken seriously, the condition of our broken world may be strong, if circumstantial evidence for why some experience difficulty with ideas about God or with belief and confidence in God. That is why I assert, believe and, were it possible, would insist that it is in relationships with each other that we meet the power behind all relationships. That means we become children of God, symbolic or otherwise, only by becoming what we are, brothers and sisters of each other. That conviction recalls the teaching of the Prophet Zechariah: "On that day, God shall be one and [finally] God's name shall be one."[20] Were we to do that work, the result may be described accurately, as a stunning, even miraculous encounter with the power of life, with God. In such efforts, we assuredly connect with others, and we may even recognize that those are wondrous *Peniel* moments of awe.

FOR FURTHER REFLECTION:

1. What role does humor play in your spiritual journey?
2. How can your actions bring a bit of "Godness" into the lives of others and into your own life?

CHAPTER 16

Partnering with God

God cannot do the work of God, without our help.

M Y HOPE IS THAT the conversation thus far confirms or adds to the notion that it is possible to have a positive conversation on ideas about God. Unlike so much that passes for debate in contemporary political discourse, we need not be stuck in polemical exchanges between only two contending and extreme positions. No wiggle room allowed, you are, in this instance, either for or against God, as our soundbite "culture" has reduced not only attention spans but also our capacity and/or interest to reflect about ideas, let alone engage in introspection about their implications for us.

Such recalls a commentary about Martin Buber, whose challenging writings about God, whether embraced or discounted, enter rarefied air. Following one of his lectures, an older gentleman expressed disappointment. Longing to hear of something more than the God of philosophers, he asked Buber, "What about the God of Abraham, Isaac, and Jacob?" In short, he wanted more than cerebral abstraction; he sought a personal context and, likely, connection.[1]

I love to imagine that Buber had this challenge in mind when, years later in New York, he gave a series of talks, published with the title *At the Turning*: "The true meaning of love of one's neighbor is not that it is a command, but that through it and in it we meet God."[2] I suspect that reflection would satisfy his questioner as it provides a path to an intimate encounter with the God of the Patriarchs.

Philosophical ruminations may demonstrate sophistication of thought, but what difference does that make? From Unmoved Mover and the flight of the alone to the Alone,[3] to the conviction that God is a word without referent, the challenge of Buber's interlocutor remains. William James precisely describes the matter when he informs us , "A difference that makes no difference is no difference at all."[4] And certainly Buber's suggestion about meeting God in others makes a difference and maybe even a different world.

With that challenge in mind, recall the discussion in Chapter 10, which pointed to an earlier time when theologians spoke confidently about proofs for God. These are best considered arguments rather than incontrovertible evidence. I would argue, nevertheless, that there is a proof for Deity's existence, even perhaps for an intimate God concept that would appeal to Buber's interlocutor and, more immediately, to the careful reader.

To wit, *we* are proofs for whatever God we acclaim, embrace, and worship. With all their variations, disappointments, and thrills, our lives give testimony to what we consider as highest values. They are the most profound and honest witness to what our intimate and ultimate ideals, standards, and beliefs may be, even if our public expressions do not always conform to our genuine convictions or are hidden from others and ourselves.

The challenge isn't God or no God. Rather, it resides in what we recognize as truths, such that were we called upon to compromise those values, life would lose its urgency and integrity, and self-sacrifice might well be the only integrity-filled response.

What, then, represents a clear declaration of our convictions? In the answer to that challenge, we find the God of every life. Or to recall Martin Luther's declaration, "Here I stand. I cannot do otherwise."[5] There is no other choice.

Especially in our time, one might insist that no matters rise to the level of Luther's assertion and, while certainly not unique to this particular moment, the sentiment, "You've got to go along to get along," seems too often to resonate as an essential conviction. Survival for its own sake and just getting ahead seem values that determine the paths we expect to follow and, equally, to avoid.[6]

In the Woody Allen film, *Manhattan*, Allen's character tries to encourage a friend to embrace a higher standard of behavior. The friend resists the challenge and screams, "You are so self-righteous. We're just people. We're just human beings. You think you're God!" Allen's character responds, "I gotta' model myself after someone." (I am mindful of the irony in citing Mr. Allen as a moral authority, but the point is well made.)

We *do* have to model ourselves after someone. And many traditions insist that *imitatio Dei* is more than our best response. It is an obligation. I understand that to mean that what we do brings God into the world; equally, what we do may drive God out.

There is a remarkable Midrash, based on a verse in Isaiah 43:10: "You are my witnesses." The Midrash audaciously declares, "But if you are not my witnesses, I am not, as though it were possible, God."[7]

That commentary explores one of the more extraordinary, even scandalous ideas in Jewish tradition. We are the way God gets into the world, and that is why all of us are needed. Consider this imagined conversation.

Two acquaintances meet on the street. Amid the rituals of greeting, one inquires of the other, "How are you?" Instead of the formulaic answer, the person responds honestly, describing a series of personal challenges and calamities. He concludes with a plaintive, "I don't even know to whom I can turn for help." Upon hearing that, his compatriot releases a sigh of relief. "Thank goodness, I thought you were going to ask me."

Of course, people need us, and we sometimes respond—some of us often. But the Midrash on the Isaiah verse reminds that not only people but also God asks, depends on, and needs us.

Another Isaiah text[8] includes a similarly daring assertion, although to describe it as just another passage is to understate the matter. The particular excerpt has pride of place, as the assigned reading on Yom Kippur, which is often, if imprecisely, called the holiest day of the Jewish calendar. In the midst of a gathering, heavy with ritual, the most well known of which is a twenty-five-hour[9] fast from all food and drink, our sages insist we hear an immediate corrective against any notion that perfect rituals are sufficient to manipulate the world and our place therein. The Prophet Isaiah provides a devastating critique of outward piety when combined with hypocritical intent. This is both pertinent and paradoxical, given that the congregation is engaged in ritual fasting. The Prophet intones:

Is this the fast I look for? A day of self-affliction? Bowing your head like a reed, and covering yourself with sackcloth and ashes? Is this what you call a fast . . . ? Is not this the fast I look for: to unlock the shackles of injustice, to undo the fetters of bondage, to let the oppressed go free, and to break every cruel chain? Is it not to share your bread with the hungry, and to bring the homeless poor into your house? When you see the naked, to clothe them, and never to hide yourself from your own kin?

Then shall your light blaze forth like the dawn, and your wounds shall quickly heal; your Righteous One will walk before you, the Presence of the Eternal will be your rear guard. Then, when you call, the Eternal will answer; when you cry, God will say: "Here I am."

While asserting a case for social justice, the text goes further. In Hebrew, it is only one word, "*Hineni*," and the phrase meaning, "Here I am," is the controlling expression, especially as it echoes Abraham's first "correct" response to the question that resonates throughout the Hebrew Bible. In fact, it sets the stage for the first interrogative in the Torah, as Deity inquires of Adam and Eve, "Where are you?" Abraham's immediate reply of "Hineni" vividly contrasts with that of the first couple: "They heard the voice of God walking about in the garden . . . And the man and the woman hid from the presence of God."[10]

Provocatively, the word translated as hid is a reflexive verb form, which means it may be rendered as they hid from themselves. And that is no small item, especially considering my effort to argue that we are the context or vehicle by which God awareness becomes present, manifest, and real.

Abraham's "here I am" suggests not only location but also engagement. You need me to do something. I am ready, if not already doing it. In effect, the Isaiah text argues that God's presence is found in, even more precisely within our righteous actions. In lifting another, we lift far more: we elevate others, self, and (here the outrageous, better, wonderful part) God. That, I am convinced, is what Buber must have had in mind when, as cited earlier, he offered, "[T]he true meaning of love of one's neighbor is not that it is a command from God which we are to fulfill, but that through it and in it we meet God."[11]

Another approach to this idea or ideal may turn some in religious circles against me as it involves an expanded notion of incarnation. For those unaware, in Christianity, the doctrine of incarnation refers to the belief that God took human form in the person of Jesus. However, a Jewish understanding lends itself to an additional or alternative interpretation. To offer an imprecise echo of the language in the Gospel of John,[12] God so loved the world that God put a bit of Deity in all of us. Therefore, we are urged to let it show, to let it grow. Simply put, the Rabbi of Kotzk[13] urges us to recognize that "God dwells wherever we let God in." This recalls a more contemporary suggestion from the poetry of Leonard Cohen: "There is a crack in everything; that's how the light gets in." My argument works even better by suggesting that's how the light gets out.

That lesson may be the implicit guideline in the architectural template for seating in Sephardic synagogues.[14] While most worship settings are variations on a standard order auditorium, with all seats oriented toward a stage or the worship setting equivalent, Sephardic sanctuaries are arranged with seating on at least three and, often, four sides of the room, in effect creating a theater in the round or, more accurately, in a square or rectangle. Unlike most worship environments, in which the primary experience of many attendees will be to view the back of another's head, the setting insists that one acknowledge others in the room. The intended lesson is that we are surrounded by persons with whom we share sacred stuff; part of Deity resides in that one and this one and (don't forget) in you as well.

The recipe for a full embrace of life is clear. As Rabbi Abraham Isaac Kook instructs:

Life surrounds us on all sides. When we rise, everything rises with us; when we decline, everything declines with us. When our essence is elevated, then all life's expressions, whatever they may be, are elevated . . . The ascent toward godliness . . . raises with it whatever is related to us, no matter how distant the relationship.[15]

Kook describes for all of us, including those who may be disquieted by the use of the word "God," how vital what we do really is.

Yet one cannot be unaware that our world is dominated by a focus on what's in it for me. So God needs us—so what? Why should we bother?

Enlightened or any other version of self-interest as paramount, there is still a good case to make. Not only does God need us, but also we are the beneficiaries of a substantial existential dividend. While biologists teach that animals are satisfied when their needs are met, philosophers and theologians find that insufficient for human beings: we have a need to be needed. That means happiness, or more precisely, a sense of fulfillment is best experienced in the *certainty* of being needed.

Equal to or greater than any miracle of the ordinary is the awesome assertion that God relies on us. As job descriptions go, that is nothing less than exhaustive, meaning there is no slow season or retirement plan. Every phase of life's journey overflows with innumerable opportunities for practice. Whatever we may do for a living, bringing God into the world is our life's calling. In effect, it is life calling.

Even assuming that observation to be wrong or delusional, which I do not believe, the investment in such work would transform, if not the world, at least ourselves. All that is necessary to prove the hypothesis is to do the work.

A rabbi enters heaven in a dream. Anxiously, he approaches the place in Paradise where all the great sages are spending their eternal lives. But he notices that just as they did in the world of the living, they are seated at tables studying sacred texts. The disappointed rabbi wonders, "Is that all there is to paradise?" He hears a voice responding: "You are mistaken. The sages aren't in paradise. Paradise is in the sages."

In brief, we help God by treating others compassionately. In that work, we encounter an aspect of experience that includes a transcendent dimension, one that affirms meaning. To use theological language, we may meet the God ideal, which resides at the heart of life. For some readers that conclusion may seem self-evident; others might consider it ludicrous. Nonetheless, it is a path that leads to something exquisite and to our *becoming* something exquisite. That effort means taking God seriously, and it provides us with the capacity to live life fully, meaningfully, no matter our circumstance, with a sense of awe, wonder, and sacred joy.

FOR FURTHER REFLECTION:

1. What are the elements that testify to the ultimate values in your life?
2. Do you recall moments when those values were challenged? How did you respond? Would you respond that way again?

PART 3

Taking Prayer and Poetry Seriously

PRAYER AND POETRY ARE two remarkably underutilized and exceedingly useful tools that can lead to a mind filled with astonishment, wonder, and gratitude. I believe that perspective is vital if we are to sustain lasting encounters with miracles and holiness, which I contend are keys to leading lives with meaning.

Like those who identify with a worshipping community, I regularly confront both the challenge and vitality of prayer. I am aware that others have long ago discounted prayer as, at best, a relic. And while there may not be any atheists in foxholes, a proposition probably no longer correct, few of us relate, even metaphorically, to Abraham Lincoln's compulsion to be "driven many times upon [our] knees by the overwhelming conviction that [we] had nowhere else to go." My tradition has limited familiarity with that posture, so I shall describe an alternative notion of prayer, one that offers a productive and bountiful path as a profitable spiritual thoroughfare.

Although many of us don't often make time to explore poetry, poems are another pathway to a sacred dimension, assisting us to be fully present to the miracles around and in us. That conviction serves as the lodestar for my selection of poems, which celebrate the extraordinary in what we might otherwise pass over as ordinary.

CHAPTER 17

Too Proud to Beg?

Prayer helps us stay in touch with holiness.

AVING COME THIS FAR, you may desire at least a hint of the equanimity and uplift, perchance the enlightenment, implied in the story about the sages that concluded the previous chapter. The question then becomes, what tools may be available to access that magic, especially and unlike in the story, before our exit from this world?

A small but increasing number of people find meditation to be an important instrument in that endeavor. I embrace that discipline with my own somewhat regular practice. But I am also convinced that a similarly effective and enriching path may be found in another approach, one both ancient and readily accessible to any and all practitioners.

Let's talk about prayer, the mentioning of which may engender variations of "You must be kidding—we are modern and long ago gave up such childish ideas." Whether embraced or dismissed, some presume that prayer consists of little more than an endless cycle of petition and plea. Something like, "Dear God, please let me get an A on the math test." It might work, if one also studies the material. It's like the priest's response to a baseball hitter's habit of crossing himself before every pitch. A fan asks: "Father, will that help?" The riposte, "Only if he can hit."

I imagine a portion of the resistance to prayer comes from a limited or distorted view of it. For instance, that the raison d'être for prayer is to encourage, nudge, or urge Deity to respond to our begging or, even more hubris laden, our bidding. That is far from the essence of what prayer intends. As Abraham Joshua Heschel said in a commentary:[1]

> Prayer may not bring water to parched fields, nor mend a broken bridge, nor rebuild a ruined city. But prayer can water an arid soul, mend a broken heart, rebuild a weakened will.[2]

I value prayer. But not because it includes some magic formulas to encourage or manipulate the universe to go off course for any individual, including me. Praying has a vital role if we are more fully to recognize that the common of our days is filled with awe, with wonder. Simply put, we need prayer in our lives, and we need to have a prayer life.

The reader may be aware that Jewish tradition has a prayer or blessing[3] suitable for just about every imaginable circumstance. The blessing with which one begins a meal translates as "Praised are you Eternal our God who causes the earth to bring forth bread." It's not entirely accurate. The earth does not bring forth bread. It takes our participation in partnership with God for bread to happen. Deeper still, I don't for a moment imagine that the God ideal in which I invest my life has any need to hear my prayers. In any event, why pray at all? Why not just dive into our meal, without pause or reflection, the way any animal might approach its feeding bowl, trough, or prey?

That is precisely the point. For the pause of prayer intends to remind us that eating, while it is a commonplace essential for persons to function, is nonetheless a miraculous activity. We gain the fuel our bodies and minds require. We derive sensations of taste and smell, a sensory and even sensual satisfaction, while our bodies integrate the nutrients and, remarkably, expel the residue. All of that awareness and more is possible and present in a brief moment of focus, an openness to an essential activity that we so regularly take for granted or, alternatively and better, may fail to include in any accounting of the spiritual adventure that surrounds and embraces us.

That insight, I suspect, is the not-so-subtle benefit of a Jewish tradition that urges us to recite 100 blessings a day. Such a practice makes it all the more likely that one is attuned to the endless number of wonders, far more than 100 that surround us always. With that in mind, I raise for consideration what some may view as little more than a tedious exploration. Obviously, I don't think so, albeit should you conclude differently, I hope we may have built enough goodwill to receive your dispensation or forgiveness.

The English word "prayer" comes from a Latin root, meaning to beg. It is far from a major act of confession for me to acknowledge that is not a posture or position I want to be in. The Hebrew word translated into English as "prayer" has a wholly different intention or meaning, removed from any suggestion of begging or, more politely, petitioning. *Lehitpalel* means to judge. But since it is in the reflexive verb form, it really means to judge oneself.

This does not inevitably mean self-condemnation; the concept may as readily urge us to an alternative conviction—that we too often judge ourselves not well enough. Or, as a colleague once suggested, "[One] who rises from prayer a better person, that person's prayer is answered."[4] I believe that is the essential point and benefit of a prayer life, not words or pleadings, successful or unsuccessful, but rather as a moment for arousal, awareness, or, to use the buzzword of contemporary spirituality, mindfulness. (I do not suggest "mindfulness" is a synonym for prayer. Mindfulness intends to convey a present-tense consciousness of the infinite quality hiding in the here and now; prayer is a method to attain that state of awareness. In short, mindfulness is the destination, and prayer is a path.)

A sign at a restaurant I visited recently read, "Life does not have to be perfect to be wonderful." For me, regular disciplined prayer provides an effective method of keeping that in mind, literally to remind me or us.

I have often heard people say, "I don't feel like praying," or "It's boring," or "I get no feeling when I do so." Those thoughts need to be turned on their heads. Not "I don't feel like praying," but "I need to pray in order to feel more fully and experience more clearly the wonders around and in us, the certainty that life is more, much more than a sentence to endure."

My wife and I have many interests in common, but one passion we do not share is her willingness to go into a store to look, not buy. She assures me this is a trait shared by many women, and I get no end of teasing that our son-in-law, wonderful in so many ways but a traitor in this aspect, enjoys accompanying our daughter on similar pointless (to my eyes) excursions. During a few days of vacation in Carmel, California, my wife and I wandered into a store just to look around: one of us with enthusiasm, the other more reluctantly. My looking took (maybe stretching here) all of five minutes, during which my bride had scarcely made it through the door. Rather than the invariably ineffective "Are you done yet?" I took refuge in a small section of the shop with greeting cards. My eyes fell on a card with a quote from one of my favorite poets, Wallace Stevens: "It's not every day that the world arranges itself into a poem." That's an evocative notion, save for one difficulty. I strongly disagree. The poem is always present. It's just not every day that we read it, see it, and are alert to it.

I am confident that many of us want to live with that intensity, that alertness to the wonders around and within us. An effective prayer life intends to remind us and guide us to that experience or destination. For prayer is a way to receive, recite, and even, God willing, to memorize the unspoken words of the world's ever-present poem.

More strongly stated, prayer serves as a wake-up call, one that insists our journey, be it twenty-five, fifty, 100, or more years, is worth the struggle and confusion, the disappointments and pain. Prayer insists that we can experience the holy and, even more vitally, that the holy can be imagined, touched, seen, not only by us but by others because for a time, the gift of life resides with us.

Prayer is the insistence that we must pay attention in order to rejoice in and respond to what is there about us always. It is the means to celebrate the wonder at the address called Michael, Emily, Ruth, and George and, as well, to be aware of the "not yets,"the unfinished and demanding work in my home, on my street, with the community, this country, our world. Prayer embraces and admonishes or insists, as per the Nikki Giovanni commentary cited earlier: "We are better than we think, and not quite what we want to be."[5]

Previous generations prayed because they had a sense of obligation, perhaps to their community and, more likely, to their notion of Deity. In our busy and materialistic world, prayer suffers because it isn't selling anything. Rather, it only offers centeredness, the mindfulness to know the path before us and the urgency to get going, as we too often sleepwalk through our one precious life.

Prayer provides awareness and clarity. Recall Gerald Manley Hopkins' reminder that "[t]he world is charged with the grandeur of God."[6] Even should we be uncertain about God, I embrace and wish to hold fast to the certainty that the world is charged with grandeur, wonder, and awe.

We can wake up, stay alert, perhaps especially on the occasions when we pray together, worship with each other. Engaging in communal prayer enhances the prospect of a personal encounter with one's best self and/ or with the divine and offers the help of a communal response to boost or provide a positive outcome to our efforts. In short, we may lift up others and also be lifted, inspired with and by them.

I do not believe that any God worth having needs or requires prayer. In the deepest sense, prayer is not directed to an entity separate and apart from us. More practically, prayer works, and prayers are answered when we are saved from the mundane of experience; prayer helps us to recognize that there is no such thing as mundane. Our task is to celebrate, share, and increase the wonder that embraces us, if only it wouldn't let us go, for then we understand that this journey is infinitely valuable.

To use religious language, when we arrive at that Sinai-like mountain top or behold a burning bush, even if it be only metaphor, our faces, like the face of Moses, may shine with wholeness, with holiness, as we abide in that moment, surrounded by a "yes" for which no elaboration is necessary or adequate. Or to recall the instruction of Emily Dickinson, "To live is so startling, it leaves but little room for other occupations."[7]

But too many of us just exist, get by, fill time, waste time, kill time. We do not celebrate our lives, at least not enough. Could we all not have more life in our living? That is the benefit of prayer, the heart of this vital skill, a gift that so many of us have given away. While a party may contain a more immediate celebration, it is an ephemeral delight. Prayer provides a more lasting return on investment.

Exercise that prayer muscle. While going about supposedly mundane or secular activities, from eating to defecating, from getting up in the morning to returning home after a long day, take a moment to breathe, to reflect, to consider. It need be no more than a moment or two of intention, a whispered litany, a liturgy whose content consists simply of "thank you." In doing so, we find, especially in the routine of daily activity, moments to rejoice and achieve a more acute awareness that we are engaged in something holy. The more you pray, the more you will find the sacred dimension in moments, and someday, may it come soon, every moment.

This wonderful and angry poem, *Sing Out*, encourages us to get to work. Its author, Aaron Zeitlin, escaped from Poland just in time to avoid being swallowed in the nightmare of the Holocaust. We would certainly understand if he chose never to invoke the divine. Yet he writes:

Praise me, says God;
I will know that you love me.
Curse me, says God;
I will know that you love me.
Sing out my graces, says God.
Raise your fist against me and revile.

Sing out my praises or revile.

Reviling is also a kind of praise, says God.

But if you sit fenced off in your apathy, says God.

If you sit entrenched in:

"I don't give a hang."

If you look at the stars and yawn,

If you see suffering and don't cry out,

If you don't praise and don't revile,

Then I created you in vain, says God.[8]

FOR FURTHER REFLECTION:

1. What gets in the way of your using prayer in the manner presented in this chapter?

2. If or when prayer "works," what happens for you or in you?

CHAPTER 18

Poetry, a Perfect Language for Prayer

Certain poems may carry us to a sacred dimension.

WHILE I'D LOVE TO imagine that our discussion about prayer will increase attendance at houses of worship, a disciplined, regular prayer life has long been, and almost certainly will remain, a minority activity. However, there is another instrument, perhaps more readily accessible, by which we may hold fast to the insights that prayer strives to convey. That instrument is poetry.

Poetry is more than words on a page. The arrangement, the rhythm, the imagery, and the insights of poems may call our attention to the awesome and wondrous dimensions of being. For a poem to work, both author and reader contribute. The text gives voice to what the reader has experienced but cannot always articulate. It brings to consciousness what the reader may know, if imprecisely, or have lost sight of over time. The poems we'll discuss here may leave one less likely to miss those endless encounters with wonder.

All poems ask is for us to be open and alert. Or, as the poet Mary Oliver says: "Instructions for living a life: Pay attention. Be astonished. Tell about it."[1]

I offer here a few poems that give me profound insight into the divine and miraculous world we inhabit. For instance, Denise Leterov's[2] "Primary Wonder" uses traditional religious language to convey a powerful, even prayerful jolt, no matter how intimate with or estranged from that vocabulary we may be:

> Days pass when I forget the mystery.
> Problems insoluble and problems offering
> their own ignored solutions
> jostle for attention, they crowd its antechamber
> along with a host of diversions, my courtiers, wearing
> their colored clothes; cap and bells.
>   And then
> once more the quiet mystery
> that there is anything, anything at all,
> let alone cosmos, joy, memory, everything,
> rather than void, and that, O Lord,
> Creator, Hallowed One, You still,
> hour by hour sustain it.

You may recall the words of E.E. Cummings:[3]

> i thank You God for most, this amazing
> day: for the leaping greenly spirits of trees
> and the blue true dream of sky; and for everything
> which is natural which is infinite which is yes
>
> (i who have died am alive again today,
> and this is the sun's birthday; this is the birth

day of life and love and wings: and of the gay
great happening illimitably earth)

how should tasting touching hearing seeing
breathing any – lifted from the no
of all nothing – human merely being
doubt unimaginable You?

(now the ears of my ears awake and
now the eyes of my eyes are opened)

It is noteworthy that Cummings, with his indifference to punctuation and capitalization, still finds it appropriate to capitalize references to Deity. That may be a clue that he really intends the magic articulated in this poem. It serves as a reminder that, as suggested earlier, there are burning bushes scattered randomly and constantly through every day. Cummings urges us to see and respond to those messages or, if not all of them, at least more than we do currently.

That brings to mind the urgency of our limited time in life, which finds confirmation and challenge in the poetry of Mary Oliver. While many of her lyrically straightforward and compelling poems focus on overwhelming encounters with wonder, none does so with more exquisite insistence than the imagery in "When Death Comes:"[4]

When death comes
like the hungry bear in autumn;
when death comes and takes all the bright coins from
his purse

to buy me and snaps the purse shut;
when death comes
like the measle-pox

when death comes
like an iceberg between the shoulder blades,

I want to step through the door full of curiosity,
wondering:
what is it going to be like, that cottage of darkness?

And therefore I look upon everything
as a brotherhood and sisterhood,
and I look upon time as no more than an idea,
and I consider eternity as another possibility,

and I think of each life as a flower, as common
as a field daisy, and as singular,

and each name a comfortable music in the mouth,
tending, as all music does, toward silence,

and each body, a lion of courage, and something
precious to the earth.

When it's over, I want to say all my life
I was a bride married to amazement.
I was the bridegroom, taking the world into my arms.

When it's over, I don't want to wonder
if I have made of my life something particular, and real.

I don't want to find myself sighing and frightened,
or full of argument.

I don't want to end up simply having visited this world.

The imagery of the last few lines, beginning with "When it's over," captures something essential and inspires even more. Oliver's reflections challenge us to be less wasteful with this "one wild and precious life," as in another of her poems, "Summer Day":[5]

> I don't know exactly what a prayer is.
> I do know how to pay attention, how to fall down
> into the grass, how to kneel down in the grass,
> how to be idle and blessed, how to stroll through the fields,
> which is what I have been doing all day.
> Tell me, what else should I have done?
> Doesn't everything die at last, and too soon?
> Tell me, what is it you plan to do with your one wild and precious
>   life?

Before leaving Oliver, I don't know if the title of her poem "Messenger"[6] intentionally invokes a Biblical context, but it has an instructive pedigree. As we saw earlier, the Hebrew word "*Malach*," commonly translated as angel, has the base meaning of messenger, which is why the Greek translation of the Bible used "*Angelos*," its linguistic equivalent. The word comes into English as angel. Theoretically, at least for the Bible, this need not require any real or imagined supernal references. Rather, it recalls my query in that earlier discussion: "Are we, perhaps, messengers who have forgotten our message?" While we may get distracted, even lost, in the busyness of getting by, this poem serves as a reminder and road map, one we should strive never to forget:

> My work is loving the world
> Here the sunflowers, there the hummingbird-
> equal seekers of sweetness.
> Here the quickening yeast; there the blue plums.
> Here the clam deep in the speckled sand.

Are my boots old? Is my coat torn?
Am I no longer young, and still not half-perfect? Let me
keep my mind on what matters,
which is my work,

which is mostly standing still and learning to be
astonished.
The phoebe, the delphinium.
The sheep in the pasture, and the pasture.
Which is mostly rejoicing, since all ingredients are here,

which is gratitude, to be given a mind and a heart
and these body-clothes,
a mouth with which to give shouts of joy
to the moth and the wren, to the sleepy dug-up clam,
telling them all, over and over, how it is
that we live forever.

Suggestions of immortality recall Wordsworth's wrestling match in *Ode: Intimations of Immortality from Recollections of Early Childhood*.[7] The poet's challenge is our problem, at least for those who would wish to live more fully, who imagine an embrace of life as a full-time passionate journey. Wordsworth laments, "Our birth is but a sleep and a forgetting." Yes, he remembers times of wonder and joy. But experience distorts that awareness and may lead to melancholy or, worse, despair. Wordsworth suggests a modest comfort in the suggestion that what is lost may be recalled in memory, even if not fully recovered.

What through radiance which was once so bright
Be now forever taken from my sight,
Though nothing can bring back the hour
Of splendour in the grass, of glory in the flower;

We will grieve not, rather find
Strength in what remains behind.[8]

Admittedly, I want to be convinced that sorrow is not the final word. I believe Wordsworth's "glory" is more than memories, be they fondly or sadly recollected. I hope, believe, and insist that "thoughts that do often lie too deep for tears"[9] need not be an inevitable or ultimate conclusion. No, the grandeur of being fully present, of being alive to our lives, means we can do and be more, can do and be better. But I am keenly aware that saying that doesn't make it true, which means I take comfort, refuge in (no surprise) another poem.

Admittedly, a forest is not the only location which may provide an environment to reorient ourselves. Yet David Wagoner's poem "Lost"[10] explores a path to recover a present tense, even connect to the constant presence of wonder.

Stand still. The trees ahead and bushes beside you
Are not lost. wherever you are is called Here,
And you must treat it as a powerful stranger,
Must ask permission to know it and be known.
The forest breathes. Listen. It answers,
I have made this place around you.
If you leave it, you may come back again, saying Here.
No two trees are the same to Raven.
No two branches are the same to Wren.
If what a tree or a bush does is lost on you,
You are surely lost. Stand still. The forest know
Where you are. You must let it find you.

The last line does give me pause, for the whole thrust of this book and, more personally, my life includes finding the path, staying upon it, and, of course, rejoicing in the journey. Perhaps, Wagoner's point is that the path is always accessible. The plea to "stand still" means to pay attention, for in so doing we find that the path to live in the present includes an encounter with presence. The dividends from that experience or awakening enhance our capacity to find cause for surprise, exuberance, and joy. That brings to mind a comment by the great naturalist John Burroughs. "If you want to see something different, take the same walk you took yesterday."[11] But I am far from alone in the insistence that one need not wait that long. The walk changes as we take it, and so do we. The assertion that the only constant is change is attributed to the Greek philosopher Heraclitus.[12] Or, as my teacher would instruct, "You cannot step into the same river twice," as the river and the person share one constant—change. For this exploration, that means everything is always renewed or, more precisely, new.

In *Sabbaths 1979 I,* Wendell Berry reflects on the obstacles that make it difficult for us to stay on point as we move through our lives:[13]

> I go among the trees and sit still
> All my stirring becomes quiet
> around me like circles on water.
> My tasks lie in their places
> where I left them, asleep like cattle.
>
> Then what is afraid of me comes
> and lives a while in my sight.
> What it fears in me leaves me,
> and the fear of me leaves it.
> It sings, and I hear its song.
>
> After days of labor,
> mute in my consternations,
> I hear my song at last,
> and I sing it. As we sing,
> the day turns, the trees move.

The poem touches the beauty and pain in all of us, even should we frequently construct walls of denial. But when we summon the courage, in whatever circumstance, to genuinely embrace our lives, the result may be an ecstasy in which distinctions diminish, if not disappear, and we become more aware of the so-much-more-than-words that we are.

In David Whyte's *The Opening of Eyes*,[14] the concluding stanza not only echoes the burning bush moment for Moses but also may lead us to a similar awareness.

> That day I saw beneath dark clouds
> the passing light over the water
> and I heard the voice of the world speak out,
> I knew then, as I had before,
> life is no passing memory of what has been
> nor the remaining pages in a great book
> waiting to be read.
>
> It is the opening of eyes long closed.
> It is the vision of far-off things
> seen for the silence they hold.
> It is the heart after years
> of secret conversing
> speaking out loud in the clear air.

While we may experience the world as "solid ground," every mystical tradition asserts an additional or different understanding. The great fifteenth-century Indian poet, Kabir, offers:

> Between the conscious and the unconscious the mind has put up a
> swing:
> all creatures, even the supernovas, sway between these two trees,
> and it never winds down.

Angels, animals, humans, insects by the millions, also the wheeling
    sun and moon;
ages go by, and it goes on.

Everything is swinging: heaven, earth, water, fire, and the secret one
slowly growing a body.
Kabir saw that for fifteen seconds, and it made him a servant for life.[15]

The poem's few lines precisely capture what has taken me far more effort
to approximate, which may attest to the wisdom in the poet's name. Kabir
comes from the Arabic, *Al Kabir*, meaning the Great.

    Before turning to a less-known author, Joseph Leftwich,[16] I suggest that
if you find references to God unwelcome in poetry, consider substituting
an alternative such as the universe, holiness, or a sacred dimension. That
effort may allow you to hear the beauty and urgency in Leftwich's words.
I believe he expresses the infinitely miraculous nature of our existence, for
whatever time and circumstance may be ours.

Death is not strange.
Strange is life,
That flesh can think,
And body believe.
That dust can sing;

That a clod
For a man's lifetime
Can house God.

That dead things live
When touched by God's breath,
Is the miracle,
Not death.

I embrace the conviction that we all have a remarkable song. It would be a shame not to sing it, to share it. Or as the Israeli poet Yehuda Amichai offers:[17]

> When I was a child I sang in the synagogue choir,
> I sang till my voice broke. I sang
> first voice and second voice. And I'll go on singing
> till my heart breaks, first heart and second heart.
> A psalm.

Finally, I offer a comment by the distinguished African American poet, Lucille Clifton: "Poetry began when somebody walked off a savanna or out of a cave and looked up at the sky with wonder and said, 'Ah-h-h!' That was the first poem."[18]

In that expression, an expletive of wonder, may be found the essential work of our lives. I offer the selections above in the conviction that the poems have a power to awaken and move us in that project. Like prayer, poetry is an instrument for reaching the divine. I rejoice in that endeavor for as long as the breath of life resides in me. I trust and, yes, pray we may share that effort together.

FOR FURTHER REFLECTION:

1. Of the poems in this chapter, which do you find most engaging? Why?
2. Which poem do you find least convincing? Why?

EPILOGUE

All or Nothing,
That's the Problem

I N CONCLUSION, I OFFER some nourishment to sustain us in the pursuit of the sacred. What follows, I believe, are realistic, reasonable, and practical items that help keep this seeker on course.

Henry James urges us to "be one of those on whom nothing is lost."[1] At first hearing, that notion sounds attractive, even compelling. But reflection places it in a more problematic category.

Taken seriously, the suggestion of an all or nothing proposition is impossible and may be an obstacle to our growth in spirit, leading to our giving up the effort in sad recognition that the goal is unattainable. I am convinced that embracing an amended version of James' statement is worthwhile. How about being among those upon whom *less* is lost? That, after all, is something attainable.

While I believe success in that endeavor yields significant dividends, the challenge remains how to reach that realistic, if modified, goal. What strategies and behaviors maximize the opportunity for success? To share a comment attributed to my wife's favorite actress, Audrey Hepburn, "I believe, every day, you should have at least one exquisite moment."[2]

One is a good start, but I am convinced we are capable of many more than just one daily encounter with awe. Here are some suggestions that may assist in becoming alert to the wonders around and in us. They come in the form of stories, which have a magical capacity to outflank our resistance to change and, even better, may enrich, guide, and inspire us.

I count myself privileged to be among those who were and remain touched by the teachings and character of rabbi Gershon Hadas,[3] of blessed memory. In fact, I am part of a large company who could not help but love this exceptional man, whom I met during my first year as a rabbi. Though he was blind when I studied with him, his spirit always shined with wisdom, kindness, and just a hint of mischief, too. And even in his darkness, his eyes continued to twinkle.

Because of his limited vision, I was one of those who would take a weekly turn reading and studying with the rabbi. Our focus was a shared passion for the body of rabbinic literature called Midrash. And while those sessions were always interesting, the real learning took place as our time together would near its conclusion. Invariably, often with a little tea or something stronger as company, the rabbi would ask a seemingly innocuous question, one that I would usually answer with what I just knew must be the correct response. How fortunate that I was frequently wrong, for I had much to learn, and he had so much wisdom to convey.

Of all his teachings, the most memorable for me began with the familiar pattern of a little something to drink and an inquiry: "Michael, when do you recite the *schecheyanu* prayer?" Having just graduated from rabbinical school, I knew the answer cold. My response was the one they teach at seminary, that the *schecheyanu* is recited when doing something for the first time or the first time in season.

For those unfamiliar with the framework of Jewish prayer, it includes an array of blessings designated for a specific circumstance. This prayer is considered a way to cultivate intention or mindfulness when embarking on a new experience. Alternatively, as part of a repetition or series, a first encounter may be enriched with the recitation of the blessing. If one never before tasted a particular fruit, in addition to the blessing for that food, one may enhance the experience by including the *schecheyanu*. Similarly, the first time in season means a setting like the festival of Hanukkah. In addition to the prescribed blessings for lighting the festival candles, the tradition adds a *schecheyanu*, but only for the first night of the holiday, the only moment that qualifies as the first time for that season.

I was confident of the correctness of my reply. But without hesitation, my Rabbi declared me wrong. Defensively, I asked, "Rabbi, that's exactly what they taught me in seminary. What do you mean wrong?"

Using a Talmudic reference, he responded, "Let your ears hear what your mouth has spoken." So I repeated my answer, although this time a little more slowly and carefully: "The *schecheyanu* is said when you are doing something for the first time or the first time in season." The rabbi's next comment changed my awareness and my life: "When are you not doing something for the first time?"

With that, a light went on, not only in my head but also in my spirit. Ever since, I hear an echo of that conversation, a voice that sounds just like the rabbi, as he whispers the Hebrew version in my ear: *Baruch atah . . . Melech haolam, shehecheyanu, v'kiy'manu, v'higiyanu laz'man hazeh.*[4] The English translation is "Praised are You, Eternal our God, Ruler of the Universe, Who has kept us in life, and sustained us, and brought us to this special moment."

Here is the amazing part. One can't get through a single *schecheyanu* before it is time for the next and the next. For what makes an experience new is far more how we see or recognize what is happening in and around us than the event itself. When we really listen to that voice, the spiritual dimension in the commonplace and ordinary, the regular and routine, is revealed to us as always new.

I heard this next story from a friend who was interned in Indonesia with her mother in a World War II Japanese prisoner of war camp. The conditions in the camp were horrendous: 80 percent of the detainees did not survive. To this day, my friend marvels that, despite this ordeal her mother continued to be a person of joy and hope throughout her long life. Less debilitating circumstances have produced bitter or cynical harvests for many people. She asked her mother to explain her continuing love affair with life. How was it possible? What was her secret?

The mother responded that even in the POW camp, she never lost sight of what she perceived to be a lifelong vocation. She meant a daily focus on a checklist of three goals which she strived to meet daily: (1) see something beautiful, (2) hear something beautiful, and (3) say something beautiful.

The application is clear, and the effect can be transformative. Despite the world around us, a too frequent catalog of disaster and despair, we should not rest until we also have done similar work. As I reflect on the story, it seems an additional item should be included, namely to *do* something beautiful.

Since hearing the story, I include those items, the original three and my addition, as part of a nightly discipline. Before retiring, I undertake an inventory of the day. Did I see, hear, say, and do something beautiful? If the answer to any one of those queries is no, I have to get out of bed because my real work is not finished.

The spiritual genius and master of Hasidism, Levi Yitzchak of Berdichev, has his own nighttime practice. The story is that every night before retiring, Levi Yitzchak would undertake a *cheshbon hanefesh*, meaning an inventory of the soul, a checklist for that day.

"Master of the Universe," he began, "today I didn't do so well. I promise that tomorrow I'm going to do better."

Immediately he would chide himself, "But Levi Yitzchak, that's what you said last night!"

"Ah, but tonight," he'd reply, "tonight I really mean it."

So often, we hem and haw or busy our way through our days, ignoring or taking for granted spiritual treasures. I like to imagine a time when, without further stalling or excuses, we insist, "This time, I really mean it." To see, hear, say, and do something beautiful every day is good homework and even better soul work. It leads us to the sacredness all around and in us and provides a confluence point for many of the ideas we've discussed above.

We *see* something beautiful when we connect with others, when we look into their faces and understand the sacred opportunity that those moments of connection provide. We *hear* something beautiful when we breathe in and out and grasp that in that simple movement of inhaling and exhaling we may hear intimations of God's most intimate name echoing within. We *say* something beautiful when we speak in deepest sincerity, offer our hearts, our efforts, and our compassion, not only in the accessible vehicles of prayer and poetry but also in our work to repair a broken person, or in the effort, however modest, to heal a fractured world. And that means we *do* something beautiful when we partner with God in making the world a place for all to savor. Because in so doing, we find the path both to savoring and, I am convinced, to saving a bit of the world as well.

This instruction of my friend's mother recalls a teaching attributed to another Hasidic master, Nachman of Bratslav.[5] Nachman teachers that a person may reach in three directions, "Up to God; out to others, and in to one's self." He urges us to understand that "the miracle of life is that in truly reaching in any one direction, one embraces all three."[6] So, when we see, hear, say, and do something beautiful, the result is that we are reaching up to God, out to others, and into oneself. And that effort leads us to be enveloped in a sacred presence that will not leave us for long or, for that matter, leave us alone.

These are far from the only spiritual exercises available. My choices produce valuable and frequent dividends for me and, I am pleased to note, for others who have taken them into their own practice. They require neither a great leap into some ethereal realm nor a retreat from the seemingly mundane matters of getting through the day. They do not claim the capacity to transform us into spiritual beings. Rather, they offer a path for our daily lives to embrace more spirit and wonder, more awe and joy, as we strive toward a sacred dimension. And we don't need to be full-time in the effort in order to enhance our spirituality and embrace a more fulsome and meaningful life. We simply reframe our encounters, be they remarkable or mundane, to focus on the spiritual adventure that is always accessible. That leads to more insight and the desire to do a little more, and then more still.

But saying that doesn't make it so. The great mathematician and religious thinker Blaise Pascal was approached by a friend who offered, "Blaise, I wish I had your faith. Then I would live as you do." Pascal's response: "Live as I do, then you will have my faith."

I make no pretense to being a Pascal, but I know that we are far more what we do than what we say.

Appendix

I OFFER THE READER THESE additional literary sources that refer to the miracles around and in us for individual reflection as we travel on our pathways toward the sacred.

From *My Bright Abyss*, by Christian Wiman:

> The greatest tragedy of human existence is not to live in time, in both senses of that phrase.

By Edward R. Murrow:[1]

> The obscure takes time to see, but the obvious takes longer.

Ferris Bueller, in *Ferris Bueller's Day Off* (Paramount Pictures, 1986):

> Life moves pretty fast. If you don't stop and look around once in a while, you could miss it.

From Rabbi Azriel's discourse in *The Dybbuk*:[2]

> God's world is great and holy. The holiest land in the world is the Land of Israel. In the Land of Israel the holiest place was the Temple, and in the temple the holiest spot was the holy of holies. (Brief pause.)

There are 70 peoples in the world. The holiest among these is the people of Israel. The holiest of the people of Israel is the tribe of Levi. In the tribe of Levi the holiest are the priests. Among the priests the holiest was the high priest. (Brief pause.)

There are 354 days[3] in the year. Among these the holidays are holy. Higher than these is the holiness of the Sabbath. Among the Sabbaths, the holiest is the Day of Atonement, the Sabbath of Sabbaths. (Brief pause.) There are 70 languages in the world. The holiest is Hebrew. Holier than all else in this language is the holy Torah, and in the Torah the holiest part is the ten Commandments. In the Ten commandments the holiest of all words is the name of God. (Brief pause.)

And once during the year, at a certain hour, these four supreme sanctites of the world were joined with one another. That was on the Day of Atonement, when the high priest would enter the holy of holies and there utter the Name of God. And because this hour was beyond measure holy and awesome, it was the time of utmost peril not only for the high priest, but for the whole of Israel. For if in this hour there had entered the mind of the high priests a false or sinful thought, the entire world would have been destroyed. (Pause.) Every spot where a man raises his eyes to heaven is a holy of holies.

Every man, having been created by God in His own image and likeness, is a high priest. Every day of a man's life is a Day of Atonement, and every word that a man speaks with sincerity is the Name of the Lord. Therefore it is that every sin and every wrong that a man commits brings the destruction of the world.

From *Ode: Intimations of Immortality from Recollections of Early Childhood*, by William Wordsworth (1770–1850):

There was a time when meadow, grove, and stream,
The earth, and every common sight,

To me did seem
Apparelled in celestial light,
The glory and the freshness of a dream.
It is not now as it hath been of yore;—
Turn whersoe'er I may,
By night or day.
The things which I have seen I now can see no more.

The Rainbow comes and goes,
And lovely is the Rose,
The Moon doth with delight
Look round her when the heavens are bare,
Waters on a starry night
Are beautiful and fair;
The sunshine is a glorious birth;
But yet I know, where'er I go,
That there hath past away a glory from the earth.

Now, while the birds thus sing a joyous song,
And while the young lambs bound
As to the tabor's sound,
To me alone there came a thought of grief:
A timely utterance gave that thought relief,
And I again am strong:
The cataracts blow their trumpets from the steep;
No more shall grief of mine the season wrong;
I hear the Echoes through the mountains throng,
The Winds come to me form the fields of sleep,
And all the earth is gay;
Land and sea
Give themselves up to jollity,
And with the heart of May

Doth every Beast keep holiday;—
Thou Child of Joy,
Shout round me, let me hear thy shouts, thou happy Shepherd-boy.

Ye blessed creatures, I have heard the call
Ye to each other make I see
The heavens laugh with you in jubilee;
My heart is at your festival,
My head hath its coronal,
The fulness of your bliss, I feel—I feel it all.
Oh evil day! if I were sullen
While Earth herself is adorning,
This sweet May-morning,
And the Children are culling
On every side,
In a thousand valleys far and wide,
Fresh flowers; while the sun shines warm,
And the Babe leaps up on his Mother's arm:—-
I hear, I hear, with joy I hear!
—But there's a Tree, of many, one,
A single field which I have looked upon,
Both of them speak of something that is gone;
The Pansy at my feet
Doth the same tale repeat:
Whither is fled the visionary gleam?
Where is it now, the glory and the dream?

Our birth is but a sleep and a forgetting:
The Soul that rises with us, our life's Star,
Hath had elsewhere its setting,
And cometh from afar:
Not in entire forgetfulness,

And not in utter nakedness,
But trailing clouds of glory do we come
From God who is our home:
Heaven lies about us in our infancy!
Shades of the prison-house begin to close
Upon the growing Boy,
But he beholds the light, and whence it flows,
He sees it in his joy;
The Youth, who daily farther from the east
Must travel, still is Nature's Priest,
And by the vision splendid
Is on his way attended;
At length the Man perceives it die away,
And fade into the light of common day.

Earth fills her lap with pleasures of her own;
Yearnings she hath in her own natural kind,
And, even with something of a Mother's mind,
And no unworthy aim,
The homely Nurse dth all she can
To make her Foster-child, her Inmate Man,
Forget the glories he hath known,
And that imperial palace whence he came.

Behold the Child among his new-born blisses,
A six years' Darling of a pigmy size!
See, where 'mid worek of his own hand he lies,
Fretted by sallies of his mother's kisses,
With light upon him from his father's eyes!
See, at his feet, some little plan or chart,
Some fragment from his dream of human life,
Shaped by himself with newly-learn{e}d art

A wedding or a festival,
A mourning or a funeral;
And this hath now his heart,
And unto this he frames his song:
Then will he fit his tongue
To dialogues of business, love, pr strife;
But it will not be long
Ere this be thrown aside,
And with new joy and pride
The little Actor cons another part;
Filling from time to time his "humorous stage"
With all the Persons, down to palsied Age,
That life brings with her in her equipage;
As if his whole vocation
Were endless imitation.

Thou, whose exterior semblance doth belie
Thy Soul's immensity;
Thou best Philosopher, who yet dost keep
Thy heritage, thou Eye among the blind,
That, deaf and silent, read'st the eternal deep,
Haunted for ever by the eternal mind,—
Mighty Prophet! Seer blest!
On whom those truths do rest,
Which we are toiling all our lives to find,
In darkness lost, the darkness of the grave;
Thou, over whom thy Immortality
Broods like the Day, a Master o'er a Slave,
A Presence which is not to be put by;
Thou little Child, yet glorious in the might
Of heaven-born freedom on thy being's height,
Why with such earnest pains dost thou provoke

The years to bring the inevitable yoke,
Thus blindly with thy blessedness at strife?
Full soon thy soul shall have her earthly freight,
And custom lie upon thee with a weight,
Heavy as frost, and deep almost as life!

O joy! that in our embers
Is something that doth live,
That Nature yet remembers
What was so fugitive!
The thought of our past years in me doth breed
Perpetual benediction: not indeed
For that which is most worthy to be blest;
Delight and liberty, the simple creed
Of Childhood, whether busy or at rest,
With new fledged hope still fluttering in his breast:—
Not for these I raise
The song of thanks and praise
But for those obstinate questionings
Of sense and outward things,
Falling from us, vanishings;
Blank misgivings of a Creature
Moving about in worlds not realised,
High instincts before which our mortal Nature
Did tremble like a guilty thing surprised:
But for those first affections,
Those shadowy recollections,
Which, be they what they may
Are yet the fountain-light of all our day,
Are yet a master-light of all our seeing;
Uphold us, cherish, and have power to make
our noisy years seem moments in the being

Of the eternal Silence; truths that wake,
To perish never;
Which neither listlessness, nor mad endeavour,
Not Man nor Boy,
Nor all that is at enmity with joy,
Can utterly abolish or destroy!
Hence in a season of calm weather
Though inland far we be,
Our Souls have sight of that immortal sea
Which brought us hither,
Can in a moment travel thither,
And see the Children sport upon the shore,
And hear the mighty waters rolling evermore.

Then sing, ye Birds, sing, sing a joyous song!
And let the young Lambs bound
As to the tabor's sound!
We in thought will join your throng,
Ye that pipe and ye that play,
Ye that through your hearts to-day
Feel the gladness of the May!
What though the radiance which was once so bright
Be now for ever taken from my sight,
Though nothing can bring back the hour
Of splendour in the grass, of glory in the flower;
We will grieve not, rather find
Strength in what remains behind;
In the primal sympathy
Which having been must ever be;
In the soothing thoughts that spring
out of human suffering;
In the faith that looks through death,

In years that bring the philosophic mind.
And O, ye Fountains, Meadows, Hills, and Groves,
Forebode not any severing of our loves!
Yet in my heart of hearts I feel your might;
i only have relinquished one delight
To live beneath your more habitual sway.
I love the Brooks which down their channels fret,
Even more than when I tripped lightly as they;
The innocent brightness of a new-born Day
Is lovely yet;
The Clouds that gather round the setting sun
Do take a sober colouring from an eye
That hath kept watch o'er man's mortality;
Thanks to the human heart by which we live,
Thanks to its tenderness, its joys, and fears,
To me the meanest flower that blows can give
Thoughts that do often lie too deep for tears.

Psalm, by Yehuda Amichai (1924–2000):[4]

A psalm of the day
a building contractor cheated me. A psalm of praise.
Plaster falls from the ceiling, the wall is sick, paint
cracking like lips.
The vines I've sat under, the fig tree-
it's all just words. the rustling of the trees
creates an illusion of God and Justice.

I dip my dry glance like bread
into the death that softens it,
always on the table in front of me.
Years ago, my life

turned my life into a revolving door.
I think about those who, in joy and success,
have gotten far ahead of me,
carried between two men for all to see
like that bunch of shiny pampered grapes
from the Promised Land,
and those who are carried off, also
between two men: wounded or dead. A psalm.

When I was a child I sang in the synagogue choir,
I sang till my voice broke. I sang
first voice and second voice. And I'll go on singing
till my heart breaks, first heart and second heart.
A psalm.

Acknowledgments

TEACHING LINKED TO THE medieval Christian mystic Meister Eckert instructs that if your only prayer were thank you, that would be enough.

In that spirit and with the recognition that there is no shortage of people to whom I cannot express sufficient gratitude, I do wish especially to acknowledge the following:

Dr. Martin Marty whose insights about the manuscript and whose teachings over many years inspire so many, including me.

Deborah Szekely, as well the staff and guests of Rancho La Puerta. Deborah, insufficiently described as a force of nature, cofounded the spirituality and retreat center affectionately described as the Ranch in 1940. For a number of years, I have been blessed to benefit from her insights and creation, as well of the innumerable and profitable interactions with the remarkable staff and guests.

Dr. Gillian Rosenberg: her clear thinking and important insights about the earlier versions of this document were invaluable for me, and I hope will prove similarly for the reader.

Beverley Slopen, book agent extraordinaire, took an unknown writer and nurtured this book and, more vitally, its author.

Ken Whyte, who established Sutherland House, which brings this book to fruition, and whose editorial comments were (why not be honest) sometimes frustrating and always, always helpful.

ACKNOWLEDGMENTS

Thank you to so many students, many of whom became my instructors, and thank you similarly and inadequately to so many exceptional teachers whose instructions I am still striving to learn, to share, and to embody.

Finally to the members and staff of Emanuel Congregation, Chicago, and the Temple, Congregation B'nai Jehudah in greater Kansas City, your embrace of me and your learning with me enrich my life more than these words convey.

Notes

INTRODUCTION

1 First presented in 1938, Wilder's play, a standard in many high school drama departments, won the Pulitzer Prize for drama that same year.

2 This is the opening line of her poem, God's World, first published in Renascence and Other Poems (Harper & Brothers, NY, 1917).

3 Composed by Mike Stoller, "Is That All There Is?" was one of Peggy Lee's (1920–2002) signature anthems.

4 From an interview with White by Israel Shenker (New York Times, July 11, 1969, p. 37).

5 From the movie Murder at the Baskervilles, featuring Arthur Wontner as the great detective (Astor Pictures, 1941).

6 Found in Portnoy's Complaint (Random House, 1969). While a major bestseller, this novel engendered considerable controversy, including that some viewed it as anti-Semitic, pornographic, or both.

7 From the French: "Le doute est un état mental désagréable, mais la certitude est ridicule."

CHAPTER 1

1 Dr. Fred Craddock, Jr. (1928–2015) was Bandy Distinguished Professor of Preaching and New Testament Emeritus in the Candler School of Theology

at Emory University. An ordained minister of the Christian Church, Disciples of Christ, he was universally regarded as a preacher and storyteller par excellence.

2 Much of this material derives from Jewish sources. That said, I am confident of parallels in many religious communities and that these specific references connect to those who may be part of another or even no tradition.

3 Numbers 22:21 ff. Every biblical citation, unless otherwise noted, employs the translation of the Jewish Publication Society.

4 Exodus 7:14 to 11:10.

5 Entitled The Ten Commandments, this movie is still a regular part of ABC television's annual Easter and Passover schedule.

6 The careful reader will notice that I didn't simply say "God said," as I can't be sure of that assertion. But it is clear that the text places this interrogative in the voice of Deity.

7 A curiosity, perhaps even a red flag or clue to pay closer attention is that in the Hebrew text the word used, Mitzrayim, does not mean Egyptians. Rather, and unequivocally, it means Egypt.

8 This is a remarkable, perhaps sui generis, moment in religious literature. "Theophany," the technical term for an encounter with God, invariably includes just a single individual or, at most, a few persons.

9 While I cannot find a record in which Dr. King offers this precise wording, it does reflect a part of his thinking, not only about the Exodus drama but also regarding the challenge of encouraging folks in the battle for civil rights in America. For instance, Rev. Dr. Alison L. Boden, in a sermon delivered on March 15, 2015, at Princeton University Chapel, links King's efforts to persuade reluctant partners that they should not join the "Let's Go Back to Egypt Committee." She elaborates: "Those original marchers were leaving Egypt . . . but some were having a problem getting Pharoah out of themselves."

10 I have long associated this comment with Heschel, but I no longer have the specific citation. It echoes a statement in George Orwell's 1984 (Penguin Group, NY, 1950, p. 81): "The Party told you to reject the evidence of your eyes and ears . . . It was [the] essential command."

11 From After, by William Blake, in Auguries of Innocence.

12 Published by Alfred A. Knopf (New York, 1927).

13 There is some question as to whether Einstein ever made this comment. Nonetheless, citations linking the statement to him go back at least to the 1940s and the writer, scientist Gilbert Fowler White.

CHAPTER 2

1 This passage is from an interview Singer gave to Elenore Lester that appeared in the October 26, 1975 edition of the New York Times (page 131).
2 Leo Rosten, in The Joys of Yiddish, defines narisshkeit as foolishness or triviality. But the nuances hint at a matter totally lacking in value.
3 This statement is the concluding part of Exodus 3:3.
4 Midrash is a catchall term for the incredibly vast body of biblical rabbinic commentary, interpretation, story, fable, allegory, parable, reflection, and more, found in Jewish tradition. The literature includes more than 1,000 years of continuing discussion and debate.
5 Bereshit Rabbah 10:6.
6 Exodus 3:3.
7 This becomes the first time that the burning bush image serves as a principal metaphor for the Jewish people, a people burned in history but not consumed. It is not an accident that so many Holocaust memorials incorporate that image to suggest the continued struggle and vitality of the survivors and their progeny.

CHAPTER 3

1 From the poem, A Normal Day!, by Mary Jean Irion. In Yes, World: A Mosaic of Meditation (R.W. Baron Publishing, 1970).
2 Rabbi Chaim Stern (1930–2001), a renowned liturgist, served for many years as the rabbi of Temple Beth El in Chappaqua, New York. This prayer and poem appears in Gates of Prayer (Central Conference of American Rabbis, NY, 1975, p. 216). The italics instruct the congregation to recite these words, along with the reader.
3 This is an excerpt from a longer poem, first published in Leaves of Grass (Fowler & Wells, 1856). According to Poets.org, the original title of the book was Poems of Perfect Miracles.
4 Excerpted from Aurora Leigh, written by Browning in 1857.
5 This is cited in several sources, including Samuel Dresner's The Jewish Dietary Laws: Their Meaning for Our Time (Rabbinical Assembly, NY, 1982, p. 41).

6 This Hebrew prayer is in every Jewish daily prayer book. The translation is mine.

7 Psalm 139:14.

8 I cannot recall the particular sage. But I remember hearing this in a lecture and, more importantly, taking it to heart.

9 From La Prisonniere, the fifth volume of Proust's In Search of Lost Time, translated to English as Remembrance of Things Past (Grassett & Gallimard, original publication 1913–1927, English publication 1922–1931).

10 Rabbi Abraham J. Twerski (1930–2021) was a prolific author with a special interest in addictive behaviors. I heard him offer this comment in a lecture, many years ago. It may be found in his book, Addictive Thinking.

11 The traditional Jewish prayer states, ". . . who causes the earth to bring forth bread." Of course, the earth only brings forth raw material for bread. So neither Deity nor humanity gets bread, unless we do our part.

12 This recalls my argument in Chapter 1, where I assigned to Heschel a suggestion about our capacity to miss the meaning of our experience.

13 Exodus 24:12.

14 Hasidism is a general designation that refers to a part of Judaism that focuses on the mystical tradition and finding a joyous aspect in the commandment system at the heart of traditional Orthodox Jewish observance. Its origins, in eighteenth-century Eastern Europe, trace to a charismatic founder, named Israel ben Eliezer, who is known to all as the Baal Shem Tov.

15 From Parabola Magazine (Winter 1997, p.49).

16 You can find this lecture on YouTube, at https://youtu.be/87DRpZ1Ac0s. The actual story is at the 6:10–7:03 mark.

17 Kafka composed 109 aphorisms. They were published, posthumously, in 1931 by Max Brod, as The Zürau Aphorisms. This is the 109th.

CHAPTER 4

1 From The Search for Signs of Intelligent Life in the Universe, which premiered on Broadway in 1977. The one-person production was written by her partner Jane Wagner.

2 From the song When the Music's Over, which is the final cut on the Door's album, Strange Days (1967).

3 Published July 12, 1999.

4 From Book 4 of the autobiographical Confessions in Thirteen Books, as it was originally called, written between 397 and 400 CE. Several modern English translations use the title The Confessions of Saint Augustine.

5 Genesis 4:1-12.

6 Groucho used this line on multiple occasions. The precise quotation is found in the October 20, 1949 edition of the Dunkirk Evening Observer, a long defunct newspaper, in a column by Erskine Johnson.

7 The Talmud is the essential compendium of Jewish law and tradition. It consists of two parts—the Mishnah (early sources) and the Gemara (later sages). There are two written versions, the Jerusalem (codified circa 400 CE) and the much larger and more authoritative Babylonian (codified circa 500 CE).

8 With all the ambivalence and damage men have historically imposed on women, the sages, alas, personify the yetzer harah as feminine and in voluptuous terms. I confess a bit of distress, as I heard this version from my Seminary Professor of Talmud. The Talmudic reference itself omits the sexual overtones. The story, as he told it, however, reflects so much of the chauvinism in early religious literature that I am hesitant to let it go.

9 From Talmudic tractate Yoma 69b.

10 On April 16, 2007, a lone gunman killed thirty-two members of the campus community and then took his own life. Giovanni made this remark at a memorial service, held at Virginia Tech on April 17, 2007.

11 From Essay III: Compensation, in Essays, by Ralph Waldo Emerson (James Munroe and Company, Boston, 1841, p. 88).

12 Rogers (1902–1987) is considered among the founders of the humanistic or client-centered approach to psychology. This quotation is from On Becoming a Person: A Therapist's View of Psychotherapy (Mariner Books, Boston, 1995, p. 17).

CHAPTER 5

1 At his trial in 399 BCE, where he chose death over exile, Socrates is credited with having said, "The unexamined life is not worth living."

2 The reference recalls Henry David Thoreau in Walden (Ticknor & Fields, Boston, 1854): "The mass of men lead lives of quiet desperation."

3 Exodus 20:12.

4 The origin of this popular phrase traces back to Jonathan Swift, spoken by the Colonel in Polite Conversation, Dialogue 2 (1738).

5 From a letter to Mr. T. W. Higginson, winter of 1877, published in The Letters of Emily Dickinson (Thomas H. Johnson, ed., Little Brown & Co., 1906, p. 316).

6 According to quoteinvestigator.com, this quote is from the September 1935 French edition of Vogue Magazine (Condé Nast, Paris, p.56). In French it reads, "La nature vous donne votre visage de vingt ans; la vie modèle votre visage de trente; mais celui de cinquante ans c'est à vous de la mériter."

7 This is my telling. An early version of the story is found in the Australian Aborigines' Advocate (June 30, 1916, Number 180, Page 7).

8 Published by HarperCollins, NY, 1974.

9 From The Essential Rumi, translations by Coleman Banks (Harper Collins, New York, 1995).

10 In Happiness Now! (Hay House, Australia, 1998). The book is no longer readily available, but the quote can be found at www.quotefancy.com.

CHAPTER 6

1 Hart was either the writer or director of some classics of American theater and film, including You Can't Take It with You, The Man Who Came to Dinner, My Fair Lady, Camelot, A Gentleman's Agreement, and A Star Is Born. See Act One: An Autobiography (Random House, New York, 1959).

2 Faithful to the quote here, I hope to avoid gender-specific pronouns elsewhere.

3 This Yiddish word means extreme self-confidence or audacity, as in the classic, albeit distasteful joke of someone who kills their parents and then asks the court's mercy for being an orphan.

CHAPTER 7

1 This is from a poem called God's Grandeur, in Poems and Prose (Penguin Classics, 1985).

2 Isaiah 6:3. The Hebrew word "kevodo," which I translate as presence, literally suggests heaviness. It is a variation on "kabed," a cognate word meaning liver,

the heaviest organ in the body. Translators commonly used the word "honor" or "glory," as more frequent alternatives to my suggestion of presence.

3 Fiddler on the Roof is a musical production from 1964 with music by Jerry Bock, lyrics by Sheldon Harnick and book by Joseph Stein.

4 I have seen this comment attributed to Ralph Waldo Emerson, Henry David Thoreau, William Morrow, and others.

5 Genesis 1:27.

6 This is my variation on a comment by Rabbi Dr. Abraham Joshua Heschel, which appears in his book, God in Search of Man: A Philosophy of Judaism (Farrar, Straus and Giroux, New York, 1955) p. 417.

7 The name Mordecai, the heroic character in the biblical Book of Esther, derives from the same root.

8 The biblical account begins in Genesis 3:1.

9 The symbol for the healing arts is often misrepresented as a caduceus, the traditional symbol of Hermes. But Hermes' staff involves two serpents wrapped around a rod. Therefore, it is more appropriately associated, as the mirror image of two snakes suggests, with trickery and magic.

10 Ironically, for the ancients the heart was more commonly associated with thinking, which gives a decidedly different nuance to the biblical phrase about Pharaoh's hard heart, in the Exodus story.

11 Golden (1902–1981) was the late editor of the North Carolina Israelite. He was also a popular author, having written For 2 Cents Plain, Only in America, and I Can Get It for You Wholesale. Rabbi Harold Kushner reproduces this story in his bestseller, When Bad Things Happen to Good People (Schocken, New York, 1981) p. 122.

12 Usually a ram's horn, it is an ancient musical instrument with a loud, sharp, and jarring sound.

13 Variations on this story are abundant among clergy. It is a favorite.

14 Rabbi Akiba is universally acknowledged as one of the outstanding sages in Jewish history. This is from the Talmud Pirke Avot, 3:18.

15 From The Faith of Helen Keller: The Life of a Great Woman, with Selections from Her Writings, edited by Jack Belck (Hallmark Editions, Kansas City, Missouri, 1967), p. 32.

CHAPTER 8

1 Wall Street Journal, June 8, 2013, from a Samuel Arbesman review of Brilliant Blunders: From Darwin to Einstein: Colossal Mistakes by Great Scientists That Changed Our Understanding of Life and the Universe (Mario Livio, Simon & Schuster, 2013).
2 From The Problems of Philosophy (Oxford University Press, 1912, p. 34).
3 Also known as Zhuangzi. From Zhuangzi and His Butterfly Dream, by Jingjing Chen, in the online publication Yearbook 2019: China Dreams at www.thechinastory.org.
4 Frederick Buechner in Wishful Thinking: A Theological ABC (Harper & Row, New York, 1973, page 31).
5 The folktale has a number of versions. Some attribute the initial version to Pablo Molinero, a Spanish philosopher and musician.
6 From The Harvard Classics (Cambridge, Mass., 1909).
7 Many cite Ralph Waldo Emerson as the source of this reflection, although the attribution remains uncertain. The full commentary can be found in Gates of Prayer (Central Conference of American Rabbis, NY, 1975), p. 240.

CHAPTER 9

1 Santa Claus Is Coming to Town was composed by J. Fred Coots and Haven Gillespie, in 1934.
2 The Sotho is a tribal or ethnic group, principally living in South Africa and Lesotho.
3 Often mispronounced with the English spelling, this name is read as if it were spelled Jobe. The Book of Job is found in the third section of the Hebrew Bible, called Ketuvim, or writings.
4 In Hebrew Scripture, rather than an alien power, Satan is considered a servant of Deity. Satan plays a role akin to that of prosecuting attorney. To avoid insinuations of "the Devil," modern translations often use the word "adversary" or "antagonist." The Hebrew makes that choice especially appropriate, as the "antagonist" is identified with the definite article "The," or "Ha" in Hebrew, rather than an assumption of a proper name.
5 William Shakespeare, King Lear, Act 4, Scene 1.

6 Job 2:4.

7 Job 2:7 as it appears in The Jewish Study Bible, edited by Adele Berlin and Marc Zvi Brettler (The Jewish Publication Society and Oxford University Press 2004).

8 Job 42:5.

9 From The Free Man's Worship, in The Independent Review 1 (December 1903, page 415–24). In 1910, Russell changed the title of the essay to A Free Man's Worship.

10 The Latin is De gustibus non est disputandum.

11 From The Spinozistic Ethics of Bertrand Russell, by Kenneth Blackwell (London, Routledge, 1985, p.6).

CHAPTER 10

1 Israel here refers to the people, not the country. See Chapter 15 for an elaboration on the origin, context, and meaning of the name Israel.

2 The author is Aaron Zeitlin (1898–1973). His personal story of having escaped from Poland in 1939 adds to the power and defiance of his composition. Originally written in Yiddish, it was translated by Rabbi Emanuel Goldsmith. I sourced this poem at www.faithhousemanhattan.org.

3 The distinction should be clear. Murder and killing are not the same. The latter suggests the possibility of justification. The former is always wrong.

4 From Chapter 3 of Pirkei d'Rabbi Eliezer, a greatly admired collection of Midrash or rabbinic commentary.

5 From the cover story in Time magazine, entitled "Science, God and Man" (December 28, 1992).

6 Charles Darwin, in The Life and Letters of Charles Darwin, edited by Francis Darwin (Basic Books, New York, 1959, p. 395).

7 From an article by Walter Isaacson, called Einstein and the Mind of God (Washington Post, April 27, 2007).

CHAPTER 11

1 Published by William Morrow and Co. (New York, 1990, page 14).

2 This word is anachronistic, if not insulting. The source from which I quote predates this understanding.

3 Exodus Rabbah 3:5.

4 In Chapter 13, I shall unpack some of the distinct aspects for what Jewish tradition often calls, simply, HaShem, The Name.

5 Many older translations use the masculine word "Lord," instead of the more gender-neutral word "Eternal."

6 I first heard this image in a lecture by Richard Rubenstein. Professor Rubenstein was often linked to a movement of theology, prominent in the sixties and seventies, called (quite imprecisely) the death of God.

7 To keep faith with the image, when the wave is no longer visible, we call it dead. But since the wave never left or disconnected from the ocean, we have a provocative basis for a discussion on death's meaning. More in Chapter 14.

8 Rabbi Levi Yitzchak of Berdichev (1740–1810) is acknowledged as one of the most beloved, exciting, and accessible teachers in Hasidic circles and beyond. The translation offered above is my own.

9 The argot of theology labels the later position as panentheism. Rabbinic tradition offers a shorthand definition . Found in Genesis Raba 68:9, we read, "God is the place of the world, but the world is not God's place" As a provocative addendum, HaMakom (the place) is one of the many Hebrew names for God.

CHAPTER 12

1 Another word for the Ten Commandments.

2 Franz Rosenzweig (1886–1929) is a German-Jewish theologian, who collaborated with Martin Buber on an historic translation of the Hebrew Bible into German. His most important book, The Star of Redemption (originally published in 1921), began with postcards sent from the front during World War I.

3 This quote is taken from a sermon called Less Is More, given by rabbi Darren Kleinberg (August 4, 2006).

4 The sages offer a depth conviction that Sinai can be any place, both this singular unique nodal moment in time, a specific time, and a symbol for the possibility of encountering God at other moments, any time.

5 The book's full title is My Bright Abyss: Meditations of a Modern Believer (Farrar, Straus & Geroux, NY, 2013, p. 146).

6 The name of the show is Religion on the Line. The flagship station is KCMO Radio in Kansas City, 710 AM and 103.7 FM.

7 According to a multitude of sources, St. Augustin said, "Si comprehendus, non est Deus." See October 4, 2021 from www.thinkingfaith.org.

8 In this context, Jew is an anachronistic term, likely of Roman origin. I use it here in reference to the people who understand themselves as connected to the Hebrews, Israelites, 12 Tribes, Children of Abraham, and Tribes of Jacob, in other words, the particular folk of Hebrew Scripture.

9 Tanakh is an acronym for the Hebrew Bible or what some in Christian tradition call the Old Testament.

10 Also from My Bright Abyss.

11 From Jeremiah 20:9. The full quote is "I thought, 'I will not mention Him,' . . . but [His word] was like a raging fire in my heart, shut up in my bones; I could not hold it in."

CHAPTER 13

1 Genesis 4:1. The Hebrew pronunciation for Cain is Kayin, which connects to Kaniti, a verb form for acquired or made.

2 See Chapter 2.

3 Exodus 3:14. Tradition suggests Moses raises at least five different protests or reasons to reject the assignment, as we know, to no avail.

4 As quoted in Carlo Rovelli's gem, Seven Brief Lessons on Physics (Riverhead Books, NY, 2016), Einstein, in a sympathy note to the sister of a dear friend, writes, "People like us, who believe in physics, know that the distinction made between past, present, and future is nothing more than a persistent, stubborn illusion."

5 Rabbi Lawrence Kushner, in Tikkun (Volume 7, No.3, p. 49).

6 The plural for shofar, the ancient musical instrument whose jarring sound is often compared to a spiritual alarm clock, which calls us to wake up and be alert.

7 From S. (Shloyme) Ansky's The Dybbuk and Other Great Yiddish Plays, written circa 1914 and first performed in 1920. Both in reference to humanity and Deity, I'd love to imagine that were the playwright alive today, he would embrace greater sensitivity to inclusion.

8 The full text of rabbi Azriel's speech may be found in the appendix of this book.

9 See Chapter 15 for an explanation on this.

10 See Chapter 15 for an elaboration of Kook's effort to reframe the meaning of the name "Israel."

CHAPTER 14

1 From the poem, The Light of Asia, by Sir Edwin Arnold (J. R. Osgood & Co., Boston, 1885).

2 Provocatively, but not surprisingly, the Hebrew word for "the place," Hamakom, is another of the tradition's names for Deity.

3 Genesis 28:10-17.

4 Recall that the English word "angel" comes from the Greek "angelos," which is a translation of the Hebrew for messenger, "malach." See Chapter 15 for an elaboration.

5 The specific wording is from The Online Biology Book, by Dr. Machal J. Farabee, in the section called Laws of Thermodynamics (September 2006).

6 Unsurprisingly, one may find substantial parallels in a variety of religious reflections between theological ruminations and scientific reasoning, including Kabbalah, Jewish mysticism's depth exploration. In that discipline, the highest expression of God is conveyed in the Hebrew word, "Ayin," which means nothing, as in God is no thing, only the energy that resides at the core of life, the heartbeat of all living.

7 A Kopek is an extremely small unit of Russian currency, much less than a North American penny.

CHAPTER 15

1 The author is Norman Gershman (Syracuse University Press, 2008).

2 Genesis 32:23.

3 The prophet Hosea (12:3-4) records the first reference to the encounter as being with an Angel, perhaps masquerading as an ish, a man.

4 Genesis 32:29 and 31.

5 Genesis 33:10.

6 Genesis 32:31. Translations distort the Hebrew with a circumlocution, as the Hebrew for "beings divine" means nothing more or less than God.

7 Rabbi Abraham Isaac Kook served as the first Ashkenazic Chief Rabbi of British Mandatory Palestine.

8 Rabbi Kook connects Yisrael with Yashir . . . El, to arrive at the translation above.

9 From the poem The Marriage of Heaven and Hell (1790).

10 From Judges, 6:11.

11 The Hebrew word for sign is "Ot," literally meaning a sign or letter. Recalling Chapter 1, it is one of several words used for what we so nonchalantly translate as miracle.

12 The original form of this reference is, "Man is a messenger who has forgotten his message," attributed to Rabbi Abraham Joshua Heschel. Quoted in I Asked for Wonder (Crossroad Publishing, Chestnut Ridge, NY, 1986).

13 By Yaffa Eliach (Oxford University Press, New York, 1982, page 79).

14 The phrase is in quotation marks as it echoes one of the few euphemisms in Jewish tradition for died. The word "niftar" literally means to be discharged from duty, which makes sense only when and if we report for duty. Perhaps, at least as a metaphor, we may earn an honorable discharge.

15 Deuteronomy 4:3, 7:19, 11:7, 29:2.

16 Deuteronomy 29:1-4.

17 The commentary is adapted from the Art Scroll series of rabbinic commentaries on the Torah. Humor aside, all three sages mentioned are associated with esoteric and mystical teachings.

18 This recalls the Willa Cather quotation in Chapter 1 of this book, from Death Comes for the Archbishop (Alfred A. Knopf, New York, 1927)

19 Leviticus 20:26.

20 Zechariah 14:9.

CHAPTER 16

1 This story, whose source I no longer recall, has long circulated in the lore about Buber.

2 At the Turning: Three Addresses on Judaism (Farrar Straus and Young, New York, 195, p. 43).

3 Unmoved Mover is at the heart of Aristotle's definition of God. The neo-Platonic and pre-Christian mystic Plotinus discusses the Flight of the alone to the Alone, the later being his word for God.

4 William James (1842–1910) was an American philosopher and a pioneering psychologist.

5 Luther offered this memorable declaration to principle as he defended himself before the Holy Roman Emperor Charles the Fifth, at the Diet of Worms, in April 1521.

6 The elaboration of this commentary may be found in Chapter 8. The complete quotation comes from Gates of Prayer (Central Conference of American Rabbis, NY, 1975), p. 240.

7 From the collection called Pesikta De Rav Kahana, the comment is attributed to Rabbi Shimon bar Yochai.

8 Isaiah 58:1-9.

9 The notion of fasting for twenty-five hours is a short-hand guarantee that one will fast for at least twenty-four.

10 Genesis 3:8.

11 At the Turning (Farrar, Straus and Young, New York, 1952, p. 43).

12 Gospel of John, 3:16. "God so loved the world that God gave His only begotten son that we might know eternal life."

13 Rabbi Menachem Mendel of Kotzk was one of the early masters of Hasidism.

14 Sephardic refers to congregations and Jews who trace their origin to pre-1492 Andalusia. Sepahrad is Hebrew for Spain.

15 Found in Congregation Brith Shalom's Kabbalat Shabbat and Evening Service prayer book (version 2.1, May 2007), written by Rabbi Baruch Halevi.

CHAPTER 17

1 See also I Asked for Wonder (Crossroad Publishing, Chestnut Ridge, NY, 1986), a Heschel compilation edited by his student, Rabbi Samuel Dresner.
2 From Gates of Prayer (Central Conference of American Rabbis, NY, 1975, p. 152).
3 For this discussion, prayer and blessing aren't only synonyms; they carry the same intent and meaning.
4 Rabbi Morris Adler was murdered on the pulpit of Shaarei Zedek Synagogue, in Detroit, Michigan, in 1966. The comment, updated by me for language, is found in The Voice Still Speaks (Bloch Publishing, NY, 1969).
5 This remark was made at a memorial service, held at Virginia Tech on April 17, 2007.
6 From the poem God's Grandeur, in Poems and Prose (Penguin Classics, 1985).
7 Letter to Mr. T. W. Higginson, 1877, from The Letters of Emily Dickinson (Thomas H. Johnson, ed., Little Brown & Co., 1906, p. 316).
8 The author is Aaron Zeitlin (1898–1973). His personal story of having escaped from Poland in 1939 adds to the power and defiance of his composition. I sourced this poem at www.faithhousemanhattan.org.

CHAPTER 18

1 Mary Oliver (1935–2019) is a Pulitzer Prize and National Book Award winner. Her poems evoke the natural world and its wonders. From "Sometimes," in Red Bird (Beacon Press, Boston, 2008).
2 Levertov (1923–1992) published more than twenty volumes of poetry and four books of prose. This poem first appeared in her collection entitled Sands of the Well (New Directions Publishing Corp, New York, 1996, p. 129).
3 Edward Estlin Cummings (1894–1962) published more than 2,900 poems. This selection first appeared in Xaipe (Oxford University Press, 1950). Reissued in 2004 by Liveright, an imprint of W. W. Norton & Company.
4 This poem is often included in the funeral liturgy for a life well lived. Originally published in New and Selected Poems (Beacon Press, Boston, 1992), I encountered it as poem 102 of Billy Collins online Library of

Congress project, Poetry 180, compiled during his tenure as America's poet laureate.

5 New and Selected Poems by Mary Oliver, Beacon Press, Boston, 1992.

6 From Thirst (Beacon Press, Boston, 2006).

7 From Poems, in Two Volumes (Longman, Hurst, Rees & Orms, London, 1807). The Ode is one of the landmark poems in English literature.

8 Wordsworth, op. cit.

9 Wordsworth, op. cit.

10 Found in Traveling Light: Collected and New Poems by David Wagoner, University of Illinois Press, 1999.

11 I have recalled this Burrough comment. I can no longer find the original citation but rabbi David Wolpe (Temple Sinai, LA) offers the same quotation and attribution in his Rosh Hashanah evening sermon, September 18, 2020.

12 A pre-Socratic philosopher. Even more precisely, you cannot step into the same river, as both it and the person are changing, which is the only constant.

13 From Berry's This Day: Sabbath Poems Collected & New, 1979-2013 (CounterPoint Press, Berkeley, CA, 2014).

14 From Songs for Coming Home (Many River Press, Langley, WA.).

15 From Kabir: Ecstatic Poems, translated by Robert Bly (Beacon Press, Boston, 2007).

16 Also known as Yoysef Leftvish (1892–1983). This poem, Death Is Not Strange, is from Years at the Ending: Poems 1892–1982 (Cornwall Books, NY, 1984, p. 42).

17 For the complete poem, Psalm, see the appendix. From The Selected Poetry of Yehuda Amichai, edited and translated from the Hebrew by Chana Bloch and Stephen Mitchell (Harper Collins, New York, 1992, p 92).

18 Lucille Clifton (1936–2010) served as Poet Laureate of Maryland from 1974–1985. From Blessing the Boats: New and Selected Poems, 1988–2000 (BOA, Ltd. Rochester, NY, 2000) won the National Book Award for Poetry in 2000.

EPILOGUE

1 The Art of Fiction, by Henry James, was first published in Longman's Magazine (September 4, 1884).

2 Found at fueldabook.com/great-advice-177.

3 Rabbi Hadas was the senior rabbi of Congregation Beth Shalom in Kansas City, Missouri, from 1929 to 1961. He served as Rabbi Emeritus until his death in 1980.

4 The complete Hebrew prayer includes names for God. In keeping with a long-standing Jewish tradition that insists on only invoking those names in sacred moments, I have inserted an ellipsis where the names would go.

5 Nachman of Bratslav (1772–1810) was a great-grandson of the Baal Shem Tov, the founder of Hasidism. His teachings continue to inspire many in the Bratslav Hasidic community and beyond. See Tormented Master, by Arthur Green (Jewish Lights Publishing, Woodstock, Vermont, 1992).

6 From christinenachmann.net.

APPENDIX

1 "Wit and Wisdom" in The Week (January 8, 2015).

2 From S. (Shloyme) Ansky's The Dybbuk and Other Great Yiddish Plays, circa 1914, first performed in 1920. A film version in Yiddish was produced in 1937.

3 The number of days in a lunar year.

4 From The Selected Poetry of Yehuda Amichai, translated by Chana Bloch (The University of California Press, 1986).